PARENTING:
Its Causes
and Consequences

PARENTING:
Its Causes
and Consequences

Edited by

Lois Wladis Hoffman
The University of Michigan

Ronald Gandelman
H. Richard Schiffman
Rutgers
The State University of New Jersey

LAWRENCE ERLBAUM ASSOCIATES, PUBLISHERS
1982   Hillsdale, New Jersey

Lawrence Erlbaum Associates, Inc., Publishers
365 Broadway
Hillsdale, New Jersey 07642

Library of Congress Cataloging in Publication Data
Main entry under title:

Parenting, its causes and consequences.

   Bibliography: p.
   Includes index.
   1. Parenting–Congresses. I. Hoffman, Lois Wladis,
1929–   II. Gandelman, Ronald J. III. Schiffman,
H. Richard.
HQ755.8.P39   649'.1   81-9824
ISBN 0-89859-086-8   AACR2

Printed in the United States of America

iv

Contents

Preface

Outstanding authorities in the fields of biopsychology and child psychology have come together in this volume to provide an integration between these two approaches in examining parenting—its causes and consequences. Several of the chapters address directly the question of how biopsychology, and specifically research with non-human animals, can help us understand the interaction between parents and children. The value of the biopsychological approach in this endeavor is seen in the abstraction of principles from these data and not in direct analogy. The book stresses what is often neglected: the wide range of differences among non-human primate species and individual differences within species; the importance of attending to the *interaction* between parent and infant at each age–noting when the parent and when the infant is responsible for the nature of the relationship; and the effects of the situation on parent-child interaction for all species. The authors do not lose sight of species differences nor of the fact that the human condition is enormously different from that of other animals because of the culture which is interposed between whatever biological predispositions exist and the actual behavior. But, by attending to the complexities of non-human primate life, to the influence of ecology and to within-group status differences, certain interesting similarities to human conditions are brought out in this volume. There are important implications for both theory and methodology here that can enrich the two fields—biopsychology and child psychology.

The chapters in this volume are arranged from the more general to the more specific. The first chapter, by Robert Hinde, focuses on the overall theme: what is the interface between biopsychology and child psychology and how can each field be enhanced by the other. The same theme is picked up and expanded in Chapters 2 and 3. Chapter 2 focuses particularly on parent-infant attachment, exploring the concept theoretically and empirically. Chapter 3 explores the value of the biopsychological approach for understanding parent-infant interaction with particular attention to sex differences in parenting behavior. The fourth chapter, by Rosenblum and Sunderland, deals with the effects of ecology, particularly feeding ecology, on primate social structure and the importance of this for mother-infant interaction and the infant's own social status.

The last three chapters are more specific. The fifth chapter by Paul Mussen deals with complex cognitive effects of parenting on older children and indicates the more limited value of the psychobiological approach for understanding human processes at this level. The sixth chapter presents a literature review and describes a new empirical study of the interaction between the cry of the human infant and the psychological and behavioral responses of the caretaker. The final chapter by Moltz is the only one focussed on nonprimate animals and deals with the symbiotic relationship between mother and infant rat.

Written in nontechnical language, this book provides an important framework for understanding parenting behavior and its consequences for survival and development. Here for the first time is an attempt to integrate the two fields of psychology that have been most interested in this problem.

The editors wish to thank the Graduate School of Rutgers, the State University of New Jersey, for providing the funds for the conference from which this volume emerged.

Lois Wladis Hoffman, Ph.D.
Ronald Gandelman, Ph.D.
H. Richard Shiffman, Ph.D.

PARENTING:
Its Causes
and Consequences

Introduction

Lois Wladis Hoffman
The University of Michigan

This volume is the outgrowth of a conference held at Rutgers University in April, 1979. The conference was intended to provide an integration between biopsychology and child psychology in examining parenting—its causes and consequences. Several of the chapters, those by Hinde, Waters and Deane, Lamb and Goldberg, and Mussen, address directly the question of how biopsychology, and specifically research with nonhuman animals, can help us understand the interaction between human parents and children. It is perhaps not a coincidence that the more optimistic views, and the two chapters that report specific biopsychology research programs, focus on the mother–infant interaction. In the chapter by Mussen, on the other hand, where the focus is on complex cognitive effects of parenting on older children, on their sociopolitical attitudes specifically, the potential contribution of biopsychology is described more conservatively. Yet there is concordance among all the chapters that there is value to the biopsychological approach for the understanding of parent–child interaction if the researcher is aware of the limitations of the animal-based data. It is from the abstraction of principles from these data, and not from direct analogy, that the understanding of human parenting can be advanced.

There are, on the one hand, a number of similarities in the approach to studying mother–infant interaction among human and nonhuman primates. In both cases the researcher is examining an interaction, and this is stressed implicitly or explicitly in all of the chapters. Hinde points out in the first chapter that in examining the dynamics of a relationship there are three different questions that need to be specified: Who is responsible for the nature of the relationship at any given age, the mother or the infant; are changes in the relationship at any given age brought about by the mother's actions or the infant's; and are the differences due more to differences between mothers or to differences between infants? These questions are important whether the subjects are human or nonhuman. In his chapter Hinde also suggests methodological approaches to these questions used in nonhuman primate research that can be applied to human research as well.

In the chapter by Hinde, as well as the chapters by Lamb and Goldberg and by Rosenblum and Sunderland, the wide range of differences among the nonhuman primate species is stressed. Lamb and Goldberg, for example, point out that simplistic notions concerning hormone-behavior relationships are difficult to hold when one considers the very active parenting role of the male marmoset in contrast to other primates. All three chapters emphasize also that, in addition to differences in parenting among the various primate species, there are individual differences within species and important situational effects on the parent–child interaction. This last consideration, and particularly the effects of the feeding ecology, is the focus of the chapter by Rosenblum and Sunderland.

The human situation is distinct from other primates because of the culture that is interposed between whatever biological predispositions exist and the actual behavior displayed. This point is brought out in several chapters. Lamb and Goldberg cite empirical data in support of this position and point out, for example, that sex differences among humans vary with the amount of social pressure present. Furthermore, they are found among prepubescent children and post menopausal adults where hormonal influences are not likely to be paramount. Hinde discusses contact comfort among human infants in terms of its significance for cultural patterns and sees the cultural variations in these patterns as mediating the specific maternal behavior required to meet the infant's needs. Mussen points out that, in understanding prosocial behavior and political attitudes of children, the models their parents provide, the use of reasoning and explanation rather than the sheer assertion of power, and the social milieu are all more important than the fact that altruism may or may not have a species-survival value.

At the same time, by attending to the complexities of nonhuman primate life, to the influence of ecology, and to within-group status differences, certain interesting similarities to human conditions are brought out in this volume. Rosenblum and Sunderland, for example, trace the effects of the feeding ecology to the primate social structure and see the ecological setting and the particular social status of the mother as affecting the mother–child interaction and hence the infant himself and his relation to the group. Surely the process, if not the content, is similar among humans. Furthermore, although Rosenblum and Sunderland note the mother's conferring of her status on the infant, Hinde refers to data based on free-living baboons in South Africa, which suggest that the effect of motherhood on the female baboon's status depends on what her status in the group was before the birth. Motherhood enhances the female's status more when it was previously low. It is interesting that this pattern has also been observed among humans; maternity increases the status of low-status women (Hoffman & Hoffman, 1973).

One of the themes of the volume has to do with the complexities of analysis in general and specifically with the complexities of the mother–child interaction. The concept of attachment, derived as it is from Bowlby's ethologically based theory, is particularly germane to the issues here. Attachment is the particular focus of the chapter by Waters and Deane. These authors review the major theories—psychoanalytic, social learning theory, and ethological attachment—and discuss three process models used to analyze the mother–infant interaction: trait models, behavioral system models, and relationship models. Trait models, discussed and criticized by Hinde also, tend to focus on individual characteristics that are assumed to explain a variety of behaviors. Behavioral system models center on the system underlying the structure of behavior and attempt to describe "the mechanisms that organize behavior and contribute both stability and flexibility." Relationship models emphasize "interactive and dyadic" aspects of the relationship and the context, including previous interactions, in which behavior occurs. Each of the theories could be explored by each of the models. The concept of attachment is defended in this chapter as in Hinde's, also. Both chapters reply to the critiques of the concept, and Waters and Deane review data supporting its usefulness.

A particular aspect of the attachment interaction, the mother's response to the infant's cries, is explored more fully in the chapter by Wiesenfeld and Malatesta. Their research involves the direct physiological monitoring of the caregiver's autonomic nervous system arousal during stimulation by the sound of the infant's cries. The interactive nature of the relationship is stressed in this chapter too as the researchers consider both the quality of the cry and the differences in response patterns of different caretakers.

The chapter by Moltz is more specific than the others and is the only one focused on nonprimate animals. The problem investigated is relevant to all mammals, however: although *Escherichia coli* is a gram-negative aerobe, pathogenic, that normally inhabits the mammalian gut, the young are not chronically afflicted with necrotizing enterocolitis. A series of experiments is described to illuminate the symbiotic relationship between mother and infant rat that serves to defend the young against enteric infection.

The book as a whole makes an important contribution to the integration of two disparate areas of specialization in psychology. The apparent antagonism between theories that emphasize socialization effects and those that emphasize biopsychological processes and between researchers who work with animals and those who work with humans seems diminished by the various theses presented here. The antagonism seems rather to result from oversimplification of complex behavioral interaction and the failure to develop adequate models and sufficiently abstract theories. This volume represents a beginning.

4

REFERENCES

Hoffman, L. W., & Hoffman, M. L. The value of children to parents. In J. T. Fawcett (Ed.), *Psychological perspectives on fertility*. New York: Basic Books, 1973.

1 The Uses and Limitations of Studies of Nonhuman Primates for the Understanding of Human Social Development

Robert A. Hinde
M.R.C. Unit on the Development and Integration of Behaviour, Madingley, Cambridge.

In this chapter I discuss some of the ways in which studies of nonhuman primates can contribute to an understanding of parent–child interaction in man and also some of their limitations. The examples I use are dictated very much by my own interests and I can only apologize to those who would have selected differently. Because to a considerable extent I am drawing on material already published elsewhere, I can be brief.

The utility of data from nonhuman primates does not in the main come from direct comparisons between particular animal species and man, but rather from the abstraction of principles from the animal data whose applicability to the human case can then be assessed. Just because human cultures and monkey behavior patterns are so diverse, it is possible to draw any conclusion that you like about human behavior by comparing selected human cultures with selected monkey or ape species (Lehrman, 1974). Even with issues on which monkeys are all alike, there are great dangers in making direct comparisons.

Let me exemplify that view from the particular case of contact comfort. All monkeys and apes spend a great part of their early lives in physical contact with another individual. But this ubiquity of physical contact between mother and infant in other primate species does not, of course, mean that human babies *must* have nearly continuous physical contact with an adult. In many cultures they do and, equally, in many cultures they do not. In each society a whole complex of practices has grown up through the joint action of biological and cultural forces to become more or less standardized to meet the baby's needs. I am not saying that contact comfort is irrelevant to the human infant, but that one must compare those *complexes* of practices in the context in which they occur rather than independent aspects of child care. It is indeed the case that the ubiquity of bodily

5

contact between infant and caregiver in nonhuman primates does give a certain perspective to some facts about human babies—for instance, that swaddling and rocking soothe, and how children become attached to blankets, and the efficacy of the pacifier. Observations on cultures in which babies are carried in near continuous contact with their mothers indicate that many infant reflexes function to readjust the position on the mother, and so on. So even such trite universals as contact comfort are worth studying if they integrate a number of facets of infant development. But one must not transpose the animal data directly to the human case.

The main thrust of what I am saying is concerned with the fact that parent and child interact within a *relationship*. This raises a number of important issues about which data from nonhuman primates can contribute. Let us first consider a few issues about the nature of relationships in general and then focus in on the parent–infant case. At the behavioral level, a relationship between two individuals (an interpersonal relationship) involves a series of interactions in time between two individuals who are known to each other. The nature of a relationship is such that each interaction is influenced or may be influenced by preceding interactions and by the expectancy of interactions in the future. By an interaction I mean A does x to B and B does y back again, and so on so long as there is no major change in focus or meaning: I suggest that a more precise definition is not worth pursuing at this point. If you are going to describe an interaction between two individuals, you have got to describe what they are doing (are they kissing or fighting) and also how they are doing it (are they kissing dutifully or passionately or perfunctorally or what have you). If you are going to describe a relationship, you must describe the content and quality of the interactions and also how those interactions are patterned. I will come back to this question of patterning in a moment, but as a trivial example, if you have a couple who always kiss after they fight, they have a very different relationship from a couple who always fight after they kiss, even though the total amounts of fighting and kissing are the same in both cases. A consequence of this importance of patterning is that relationships have emergent properties that are not present in the individual interactions. It is of course also the case that interactions have properties that are simply not relevant to the behavior of individuals in isolation. You cannot talk about an individual in isolation as being competitive, for instance (Hinde, 1979).

In relationships between adult human beings, it goes without saying that the behavioral level is not all. The course of each interaction is influenced by our perceptions of previous interactions and our expectations about interactions in the future. We evaluate our relationships, assess both our partners and the extent to which we have ourselves behaved as we would like to have behaved, wondering whether we have created the right impression. We shall return to this later. Another point about relationships between individuals is that social behavior may provide little guide to the existence or formation of social relationships, and one must make a clear distinction between the two. In our own studies of nursery school children we have been using categories of social participation based on those of Parten (1932)—that is self-play, parallel play, group play, and interactive play (Roper and Hinde, 1978). And at the same time, we have been assessing to what extent the children have long-term relationships with each other. These are 3½-to 4½-year-old children and our criterion that two children have a relationship with each other is that they spend more than a certain percentage of the observation time sitting next to each other. (We justify that as being an adequate measure of friendship because we can show that the more often they sit next to each other, the more likely they are to interact with each other when they are sitting next to each other). You might expect that children who show a lot of self-play (that is who play a lot on their own) would not have good friends. And furthermore, you might expect that children who show a lot of parallel play (that is, who do not interact very much with the children they are sitting next to) would not have so many good friends as those who show much group and interactive play. The data did not really support such predictions. There was a tendency in that direction, but there were some children who showed a lot of self-play who also had good friends, and there were many children who often sat next to each other but seemed to interact only seldom when they were doing so (Hinde, 1978).

All that this is saying is what we know already, that you can be sociable and yet direct your social behavior promiscuously; and you can be devoted but not overtly sociable. It is thus important to distinguish between social behavior and social relationships.

Another point about relationships in general is that if you are going to understand relationships between individuals you have got to come to terms with dialectics of two types (Fig. 1. 1). One is a dialectic between personality and relationships. The properties of every interpersonal relationship are affected by the personalities of the individuals involved. But at the same time our personalities are affected by the relationships that we have experienced. Of course this is especially the case with young children, but to some extent it is true throughout life. There is a real sense in which we are those that we love and have loved—and hated. So the student of interpersonal relationships has got to come to terms with a dialectic between personality and relationship.

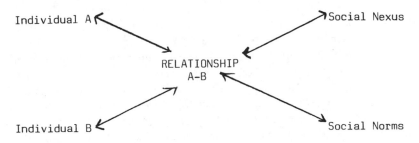

FIG. 1.1.   Relationships seen as involving dialectics with the personalities of the individuals concerned and with the social situation.

He also must come to terms with the dialectic between the relationship and the social situation: each participant in a relationship also has relationships with other individuals which affect the relationship in question, and furthermore each individual is affected by social norms determined by the culture that, again, affect the nature of that relationship. Conversely the social nexuses in which the relationships are situated and the social norms that govern their course are transmitted and transmuted through the agency of relationships.

Now over all these issues I suggest that data from nonhuman primates can *help,* though of course they cannot provide *all* the answers. One consequence of thinking about parent and child as involved in a relationship is that one must recognize that virtually all the measures one takes of parent and offspring interacting are measures of the relationship and not of either parent or offspring independently. Some studies of human parent–child interaction neglected this issue. For example, consider the use of such measures as how quickly the mother goes to the baby after it stops crying as an indicator of maternal propensities or maternal characteristics, and of how much the baby cries as a measure of baby characteristics. It is clear that how much a baby cries is determined in part by what sort of mother it has; and how quickly the mother goes to the baby when it cries is determined in part by how often the baby has already cried that morning. In a similar manner every measure that one takes must be taken as in part a measure of the relationship and not solely of the propensities of one or the other individual.

That being so, in studying the dynamics of the parent–child (or any other) relationship, one must remember that one is dealing with two interacting organisms, changes in one constantly producing changes in the other. An analysis in short-term stimulus–response terms is likely to flounder. I believe that if one is going to tease apart the dynamics of the relationship it is necessary to phrase the questions that you ask very carefully. Because I have discussed this in print more than once, I can be brief.

Figure 1.2 shows four measures of mother–infant interaction in rhesus monkeys. In each case a median and interquartile range is shown. The time off the mother and the proportion of that time spent at a distance from the mother are self-explanatory. Figure 1.2c shows a measure of the frequency with which the infant is rejected by the mother in its attempts to gain contact. Figure 1.2d is a measure of the infant's role in the maintenance of proximity to the mother when it is off her, derived as follows: we recorded every time the infant approached the mother or the mother approached the infant and every time the infant left the mother or the mother left the infant, leaving or approaching being defined as crossing a 60 cm radius around the mother. Then we calculated the proportion of approaches that were due to the infant and the proportion of leavings that were due to the infant, and took the one from the other. Thus we have the proportion of approaches due to the infant minus the proportion of leavings due to the infant. If this is positive, it means that the infant is responsible for a higher proportion of

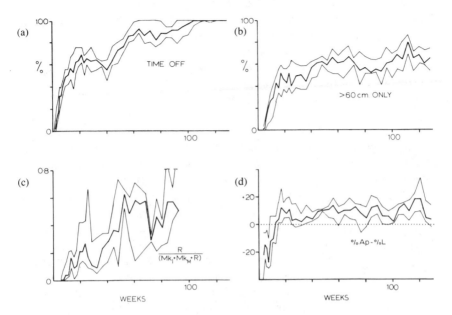

FIG. 1.2. The course of mother–infant interaction in small captive groups of rhesus monkeys. (a) Time off mother, as percentage time observed. (b) Time more than 60 cm from mother, as percentage time off. (c) Frequency with which infant was rejected by mother relative to frequency with which contact was established or infant tried to gain contact. (d) Infant's role in the maintenance of proximity. See text.

approaches than it is of leavings. If it is negative, it means that the infant is responsible for more leavings than it is approaches. And in the latter case it must be the mother who is primarily responsible for the maintenance of proximity.

Now, the first question one can ask is: at any one age is the nature of the relationship due primarily to the mother or to the infant? And this sort of measure—one can use a similar measure for contact—shows that in the early weeks the mother is primarily responsible for the maintenance of proximity, for the index is negative. Subsequently it becomes positive, and that shows that the infant is primarily responsible for the maintenance of proximity.

Second, one can ask: are the *changes* in the relationship with age due primarily to *changes* in the mother or to *changes* in the infant? To be specific, as the infant grows it spends more time off the mother. Is that change with age due more to the infant changing or to the mother changing? If it were due to the infant, you would expect the frequency of rejections to go down because, as the infant becomes more independent of the mother, the mother would have to reject it less. In fact they go up, and the infant's responsibility for the maintenance of proximity similarly goes up. This leads us to suppose that the changes with age are due more to changes in the mother than to changes in the infant.

This was a surprising finding to us because, as one watches monkeys they get bigger and more able to locomote and more interested in their social companions and in the world about them. At first sight it seems as though the changes are due to changes in the infant. But the finding that changes in the mother are primarily responsible for determining the change in the relationship is confirmed by two lines of evidence from the Madison laboratory—namely, if you rear infants on surrogate mothers, then they stay attached to those surrogate mothers to an older age than they would to their natural mothers, presumably because the surrogate mother does not reject them (Hansen, 1966). And if you rear them in peer–peer dyads, they stay attached to each other longer, presumably because each clasps the other and does not reject it (Harlow & Harlow, 1969).

I would emphasize that I am only talking about the first stage in teasing apart the nature of these changes with age. Of course the changes in the mother that are important in determining the changes in the relationship with age may be due to changes in the infant. It demands more milk, hangs on her tail or pulls her ears more, gets heavier, and so on. I am not talking about final causes but about gradually teasing apart the change in the relationship. I am aware of the work by Dr. Rosenblum and others showing that when a mother rejects an infant, that act may cause it to cling more tightly, but I regard that as a short-term effect: what I'm talking about here are long-term changes in the relationship over time.

The next question one can ask is: are the individual *differences* at any one age due more to *differences* between mothers or to *differences* between infants? One can approach this question of individual differences by generalizing the argument that I have just given in the following way. Let us suppose that there are only four things that can happen: (1) the infant can approach the mother more; (2) it can leave the mother more; (3) the mother can become more possessive of the infant; or (4) the mother can become more rejecting. Now for each of those possibilities one can make predictions about the measures of the mother–infant relationship. If the infant becomes more independent, it will spend more time off and at a distance; it will be rejected less; and it will play a smaller role in the maintenance of proximity. Similar predictions can be made for each of the four types of change. Table 1.1 shows that if the changes are due to the infant, then certain pairs of measures (time off and the relative frequency of rejections; time at a distance and %Ap – %L) move in opposite directions, but if the changes are due to the mother, they move in the same direction. So by looking at correlations between measures, one can assess whether the *changes* with age were due more to changes in the mother or more to changes in the infant. That is what we were doing just now. In the same way, at any one age you can use correlations between measures to ask whether *differences* between dyads are due more to differences between mothers or differences between infants. The correlations were not high, but they did show a clear trend from being positive early on to being negative later on. That means that the interdyad differences are due more to differences between mothers in the early weeks and more to differences between infants in later weeks.

TABLE 1.1
Predicted Directions of Change of Four Measures
of the Mother-Infant Relationship
with Four Types of Simple Change in Either Mother or Infant

			Time Off	Frequency of Rejections	Time > 60 cm from Mother	Infant's Role in Proximity
1.	M	I ←	−	+	−	+
2.	M	I →	+	−	+	−
3.	M →	I	−	−	−	−
4.	M ←	I	+	+	+	+

The important point is that answers to these three questions, Who is responsible for the nature of the relationship at any one age; are changes due more to changes in mothers or in infants; and are differences at any one age due more to differences between mothers or between infants? are *different* questions and have *different* answers. So if one is going to understand the dynamics of development of a relationship one must phrase one's questions precisely.

There is another way of tackling this sort of problem that must be mentioned, though it is now widely known. Figure 1.3 shows Clarke-Stewart's (1973) data on how much the child looks at the mother at two ages, and how much time mother and child are in the same room at two ages. By looking at correlations in all possible ways—i.e., by cross-lagged analysis—it is possible to argue that how much the child looks at the mother at age 1 affects how much the mother and child are together at the second age. There are some general difficulties with this method, useful though it can be. One is that there is an assumption of stationarity which is not necessarily met in the data. Second, there is an implication that the

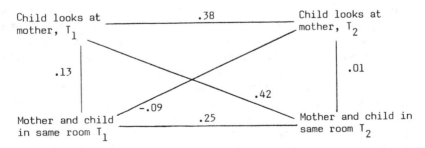

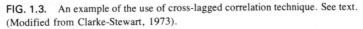

FIG. 1.3. An example of the use of cross-lagged correlation technique. See text. (Modified from Clarke-Stewart, 1973).

measures are measures of child and mother independently rather than measures of the relationship. Third, it is often difficult to interpret the pattern of correlations. I am not implying that one method is better than the other; both are useful in particular contexts.

Now I want to turn to say a quick word about the early development of the parent–child relationship. On the conceptual level, much progress has been due to John Bowlby's (1969) use of studies of imprinting and his borrowing of the concept of behavioral system from ethology. Now the concept of a behavioral system is very close to that of instinct and was used by Tinbergen, Baerends, and others to refer to a whole complex of responses serving a particular biological end. For instance Baerends' analysis of certain aspects of the behavior of herring gulls during incubation led to a picture of a behavioral system that included the motor responses and first- and second-order control systems (Baerends, 1976). In such a system the several responses bear varying relations to each other. Some are alternatives to each other; some lead to another; some inhibit each other; some facilitate each other; some share causal factors to varying degrees; some share functions; and so on. Analyses of that sort were the origin of Bowlby's concept of the behavioral system. The concept of *attachment* was derived from that of the behavioral system. It was criticized by many workers who misunderstood its nature and treated it as an intervening variable.

In an important discussion of the nature of intervening variables N. E. Miller (1959) used the following example. If you treat rats in three different ways, giving three independent variables; and if you measure their behavior in three different ways, giving three dependent variables, nine relations between independent and dependent variables must be established if you want to understand the whole system. But if you can put *thirst* in the middle, as an intervening variable, there are only six relationships to be established. In such a case thirst as an intervening variable provides economy. However it is useful only insofar as you are interested in the extent to which the three dependent variables are correlated with each other. As soon as you become interested in the extent to which they depart from correlation, thirst ceases to be a useful intervening variable. In the present context it was argued that the various measures of attachment did not show high intercorrelations and, therefore, that attachment was not a useful concept. Although this would be a valid criticism if attachment were used as an intervening variable, it is naive if you understand the nature of a behavioral system. This is an issue that Sroufe and Waters (1977) have dealt with admirably in a recent paper, though without, if I may say so, giving adequate recognition to the biological origins of the concept of attachment.

There is, however, one problem that still remains, a conceptual problem. The concept of attachment, arising from that of a behavioral system here seen as serving to promote proximity with the caregiver, applies to one half of the dyad, the infant. The mother's behavioral system is very different from that of the infant. But when attachment is measured, it is usually measured with the

Ainsworth Strange Situation technique (Ainsworth, Salter, Blehar, Waters, & Wall, 1978). Those who use this technique usually refer to the results as providing a categorization of *infants,* who are said to be securely attached, anxiously attached, and so on. But what is measured is surely the relationship between mother and infant and not a property of the infant or a property of the mother. In fact, using the Strange Situation technique, Main and Weston (1981) have recently shown that infants behave differently with their mothers from the way in which they behave with their fathers. So it is not just a property of the infant that the Strange Situation test is measuring, it is a property of the parent–child *relationship*. This suggests that the precise nature of the attachment concept requires some further thought.

The next point I want to consider very briefly concerns the social nexus in which the infant develops. In Figure 1.4 a and c show the time infants spent off and at a distance from their mothers, for rhesus monkey dyads that were either living alone or living in a social group with a male and several females and their young, the cage size being the same in both cases. The infants spent more time

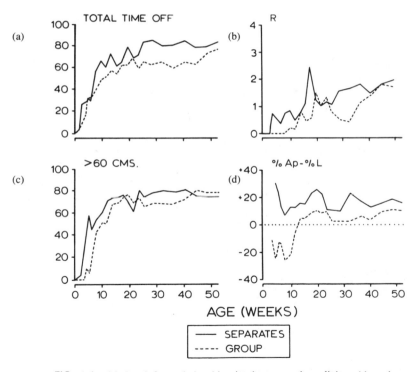

FIG. 1.4. Mother–infant relationships in rhesus monkeys living either alone (———) or in groups (---). (a) Time off mother as % of time of the observed. (b) Frequency of rejections. (c) Time > 60 cm from mother as % of time off. (d) Infant's role in maintenance of proximity.

off their mother and more of their time at a distance from their mother if they were being reared alone than if they were reared in a larger social group. That this was actually due to a difference between mothers can be seen by comparing the frequency of rejections with the time off and using the same argument as in Table 1.1. Thus the presence of social companions affects the mother–infant relationship.

Furthermore, the presence of the infant affects mother–other relationships. Figure 1.5 shows data gathered by a colleague, Robert Seyfarth (1976), on free-living baboons in South Africa. He has arranged the females in the troop in dominance order, anticlockwise. The figure shows the grooming that each female received before (above) and after (below) her infant was born. The high-ranking female (*WEL*) received much grooming before her baby was born and the birth of her baby brought little change, but the low-ranking one (*PM*) received relatively little grooming from high-ranking animals before her baby was born but much more afterwards. Thus her social relationships were much affected by the birth of the baby. Generalizing these sorts of data leads us to the

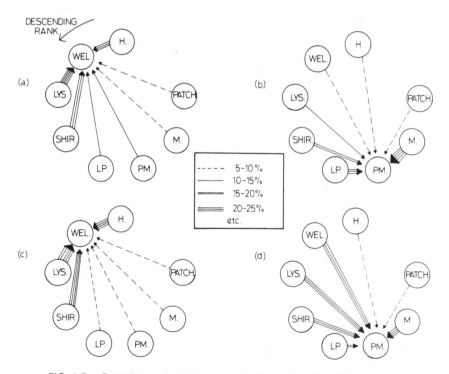

FIG. 1.5.   Grooming received by two females in a troop of free-living baboons before (upper) and after (below) the births of their babies. Females are arranged anticlockwise in order of dominance. (R. M. Seyfarth, 1976).

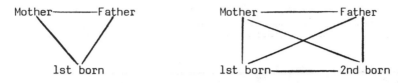

FIG. 1.6.   The increase in the complexity of a family on the arrival of the second child.

view that one must think of a social group as involving a set of relationships in which every relationship affects every other one.

Turning to the human case, Dunn and Kendrick (1981) have been studying what happens in a human family when a second child is born. They studied families in which the mother was pregnant with the second child and followed them through for the next 18 months or 2 years. It is not possible here to discuss the complex effects that they found, but Fig. 1.6 shows immediately the enormous increase in the possible complexity of effects of relationships on relationships when a second child is born. At that sort of analytical level the monkey data serve as a model. But when it comes to thinking about *how* relationships in a family affect each other, it is necessary to go a long way beyond the data from nonhuman primates. One of the issues is, of course, that the mother will be influenced by social norms. She has grown up to have views about how the firstborn should behave to the secondborn, and this will affect her relationship with the firstborn. Also, if you think in balance theory terms, when the mother loves the secondborn and sees sees the father loving the secondborn, that will affect her relationship with the father. So one must think in quite different conceptual terms for the human family from those we (at present?) find useful in the nonhuman primate case.

Now, in another context I have argued that, to integrate the slightly different things in which we are all interested, we need a science of interpersonal relationships. Such a science could fill a central void in psychology between the study of personality and social psychology, child development, and even sociology. As a biologist, I believe that in order to have such a science of interpersonal relationships we need a descriptive base. Although we do not yet know exactly what to measure about interpersonal relationships, it is possible to make a list of categories of dimensions about interpersonal relationships that are important. (These are shown in Table 1.2: see Hinde, 1979 for detailed discussion). For all of these issues except the last there are instruments by which they can be measured. Some are fairly crude, but at any rate a start is being made.

In the present context I want to emphasize two things. First, what a very unusual relationship the parent–child relationship is. All the interactions are complementary. Intimacy really has very little meaning early in the parent–child relationship. Interpersonal perception is certainly one-sided. Commitment has

TABLE 1.2
Proposed Categories of Dimensions of Interpersonal Relationships

1. Content of interactions: What the participants do together.
2. Diversity of interactions: How many different things do they do together?
3. Quality of interactions: How they do what they do together.
4. Relative frequency and patterning of interactions: Properties of the relationships that arise from interactions of different types.
5. Reciprocity vs. Complementarity: The extent to which the partners show similar or different but complementary behavior in their interactions.
6. Intimacy: The extent to which the participants reveal themselves to each other.
7. Interpersonal perception: Properties concerned with the extent to which the partners perceive each other as they "really are," perceive each other to see them as they see themselves, etc.
8. Commitment: The extent to which the partners direct their behavior towards furthering the course of the relationship.

very little meaning to the child. Although the mother is much influenced by social norms—she is keen to do what Dr. Spock says or to build up a parent–child relationship that is congruent with her culture—the baby is not concerned by such issues. So the parent–child relationship, although it is often held up as the source if not the paradigm of all human interpersonal relationships, is a very odd one. And the transition from the parent–child relationship to other relationships in the individual's life must clearly be a very complex one. The second point is that there are many things here over which monkey data are clearly not going to help in any way whatsoever. You cannot use monkey data to study intimacy, interpersonal perception, commitment, and so on. But there are some issues over which the monkey data can help. For example, Dr. Michael Simpson has used data on rhesus monkeys to show how an important quality of interactions, the extent to which the behavior of the two partners is coordinated, can be measured (Hinde & Simpson, 1975). And it has also proved possible to use monkey data to explore the properties of ratio measures (e.g., the frequency with which an infant's attempts to gain the nipple are rejected *relative to* the total number of attempts) and to show that such measures can reveal something more than, or something different from, the absolute measures on which they are based (Hinde & Hermann, 1977).

    In conclusion, then, I would suggest that there are many ways in which studies of nonhuman primates can be very revealing about human social development. But of course primatologists-ethologists can not solve all the problems that arise in the human case. People function at cognitive and moral levels different from those of monkeys; techniques and concepts appropriate to their level of functioning are essential. This is a statement of the obvious, but it is sometimes easy to assume that an approach powerful in one context will be ubiquitously so.

REFERENCES

Ainsworth, M. D. Salter, Blehar, M. C., Waters, E., & Wall, S. *Patterns of Attachment* (A Psychological Study of the Strange Situation.) Hillsdale, N.J.: Lawrence Erlbaum Associates, 1978.

Baerends, G. P. The functional organization of behavior. *Animal Behavior, 24,* 726–738, 1976.

Bowlby, J. *Attachment and Loss* (Vol. 1, Attachment). London: Hogarth, 1969.

Clarke-Stewart, K. A. Interactions between mothers and their children: characteristics and consequences. *Monographs of the Society for Research in Child Development, 38,* No. 6-7, 1973.

Dunn, J. and Kendrick, C. The arrival of a sibling: changes in patterns of interaction between mother and first born child. *Journal of Child Psychology and Psychiatry, 21,* 119–132, 1980.

Harlow, H. F., & Harlow, M. K. Effects of various mother–infant relationships on rhesus monkey behaviors. In B. M. Foss (Ed.) *Determinants of Infant Behaviour* (Vol. 4). London: Methuen, 1969.

Hansen, E. W. The development of maternal and infant behavior in the rhesus monkey. *Behaviour, 27,* 107–149, 1966.

Hinde, R. A. Interpersonal relationships—In quest of a science. *Psychological Medicine, 8,* 373–386, 1978.

Hinde, R. A. *Towards understanding relationships.* London: Academic Press, 1979a.

Hinde, R. A., & Hermann, J. Frequencies, Durations, Derived Measures and their Correlations in Studying Dyadic and Triadic Relationships. In H. R. Schaffer (Ed.) Studies in Mother–Infant Interaction London: Academic Press, 1977.

Hinde, R. A., & Simpson, M. J. A. Qualities of mother–infant relationships in monkeys. *Ciba Foundation Symposium 33* (new series) North Holland: Elsevier, p. 39-67, 1975.

Lehrman, D. S. Can psychiatrists use ethology? In N. F. White (Ed.) *Ethology and Psychiatry* Toronto: University of Toronto Press, 1974.

Main, M. and Weston, D. Security of attachment to mother and to father related to conflict behavior and the readiness to establish new relationships. *Child Development* (in press).

Miller, N. E. Liberalization of basic S–R concepts. In S. Koch (Ed.) *Psychology, a Study of a Science,* Study 1, (Vol. 2). New York: McGraw-Hill, 1959.

Parten, M. B. Social participation among preschool children. *Journal of Abnormal and Social Psychology, 27,* 243–269, 1932.

Roper, R., & Hinde, R. A. Social behavior in a play group: consistency and complexity. *Child Development, 49,* 570–579, 1978.

Seyfarth, R. Social relationships among adult female baboons. *Animal Behaviour, 24,* 917–938.

Sroufe, L. A., & Waters, E. Attachment as an organizational construct. *Child Development, 48,* 1184–1199, 1977.

2

Infant–Mother Attachment: Theories, Models, Recent Data, and Some Tasks for Comparative Developmental Analysis

Everett Waters
Kathleen E. Deane
State University of New York at Stony Brook

Parental investment is an elegant behavioral strategy with significant long-term as well as short-term consequences. In the long term the goal or predictable outcome of parental behavior is usually some degree of reproductive success among one's offspring. In the short term one major goal or predictable outcome is a species-specific pattern of infant–adult bond or attachment. In some species the primary function of an infant–adult bond is to afford protection from predation. In primates and especially humans patterns of attachment are also important in the development of social and cognitive competence. In all species both survival and behavioral/reproductive competence are necessary for reproductive success. Thus, in this sense, the short-term consequences of parental behavior provide the vehicle or mechanisms through which the long-term consequences can be realized.

This chapter focuses upon the infant–mother bond in humans. In the first section we review three major theoretical perspectives from which this phenomenon has been approached. This is followed by an outline of three process models that have been used in analyses of the infant–mother tie. We summarize several critiques of the attachment construct in a subsequent section and present empirical replies to these critiques. This entails a summary of selected recent research on relationships between neonatal behavior, infant–mother interaction, environmental stress, peer relations, and patterns of attachment. In conclusion we briefly attempt to identify theoretical and empirical issues that are important for integrative comparative analyses of attachment relationships as important consequences and determinants of parental behavior.

THEORIES OF THE INFANT–MOTHER TIE

Psychoanalytic theory, behavioral learning theories, and comparative ethology have inspired the major investigations of infant–mother ties in humans. Unfortunately these perspectives are not easily integrated. As world views they make rather different assumptions, set dissimilar tasks for themselves, and invoke different data bases and research tools. As a consequence there is not yet a unified theory of infant–mother ties. In fact the conceptualizations of infant–mother ties within these perspectives are different enough to warrant distinct labels, almost as if each theory referred to a different phenomenon. Psychoanalysts refer to the infant–mother bond as the primary example of *object relations*. Learning theorists have generally conceptualized infant–mother relationships in terms of behavioral *dependency*. The term *attachment* was first employed by Bowlby (1969) as an alternative to the notions of object relations and dependency. Although the term *attachment* is often used as the generic label for any research on the infant–mother bond, it specifically refers to the ethological/behavioral systems constructs developed in Bowlby's series, *Attachment and Loss* (1969, 1972).

Ainsworth (1969, 1972) has published several comprehensive reviews of attachment theory and research organized along the lines of these theoretical perspectives. This strategy tends to minimize differences within perspectives and to overlook eclectic approaches. For our present purposes, however, we maintain this distinction among perspectives in order to simplify our presentation. In addition, as we review each theory we limit our focus to three defining issues. What does each perspective assume concerning: (1) the nature of the infant's tie to its mother; (2) the origin of this tie and the mechanisms for its development; and (3) the stability or developmental significance of the infant–mother tie? The reader is referred to Ainsworth (1969, 1972), Maccoby and Masters (1970), Sroufe and Waters (1977), and Cairns (1979) for broader reviews and to Ainsworth (1973), Cairns (1979), and Rajecki, Lamb and Obmascher (1978) for closer looks at the range of differences within the three major perspectives.

The Psychoanalytic Theory of Object Relations

Nature of the Infant–Mother Tie. Psychoanalysts consider every individual to be endowed with a fixed amount of mental energy. This energy can be used to mobilize adaptive behavior, engage in a wide range of cognitive activity, and help build defenses against instinctual drives and the tendency toward immediate gratification. In addition, it can be directed outward toward objects in the environment much as attention is turned toward some objects and not others. The process or mechanism by which mental energy is directed toward or invested in another person over a period of time is called *cathexis*. Love relationships involve investment of mental resources in the formation of a cathectic bond between individuals. This implies that one person invests both attention and affect in another. In theory, cathexes of this type are never entirely withdrawn. According to Freud the infant–mother tie is not different in kind from bonds of love between adults. It is an affective bond and by virtue of being the first love relationship it is considered to be the strongest and longest lasting and in some sense to be the "prototype" of all later love relationships.

This conceptualization of the infant–mother tie as an affective bond has several important implications. First, because the energy involved is a fixed quantity, only a limited number of such bonds can be maintained at once. Insofar as the infant's dependency on its mother for all its needs is complete and its investment in her is unqualified, its tie to her should tend to be exclusive. Second, the psychoanalytic view at least suggests that the amount of energy invested in a given other differs from person to person and from relationship to relationship. This points to quantitative differences in strength of attachment as a salient dimension of individual differences. Third, the notion of an affective bond allows no direct mapping of the strength or quality of a bond into a set of behaviors. Independence does not imply indifference; clingingness does not imply confidence or unqualified positive feelings. In infants and adults alike, the strongest protest of separation or loss does not necessarily imply the strongest or deepest bond to the loved one.

The Origins of the Affective Bond.   In psychoanalytic theory, the term *object* refers to the vehicle through which instinctual drives can be discharged. Freud viewed hunger as the principal drive state with which an infant must cope. The strength of the bond to the mother was congruent with her role as the sole appropriate object through which this drive state could be reduced. Thus psychoanalytic theory has always placed great emphasis on the feeding situation as an important determinant of the infant–mother bond. In a word, the bond arises from, or in the context of, drive reduction.

Two implications of this analysis concern the range of inputs that can lead to formation of a bond and the relationship between observable maternal behavior and bond formation. Objects are generally limited in the drive states they can serve. Because this means that some inputs are more relevant than others to reduction of an infant's primary drives, it implies that some parental behaviors should have special significance for bond formation. In this context parents and psychologists alike have often wondered whether an infant can be cared for and fed by a nurse and yet form an attachment to its mother.

Harlow's well-known research with infant macaques is often cited as decisively refuting drive reduction theories that imply the infant would only become attached to its nurse. At the very least his work indicates that feeding per se was overestimated in Freud's theory. Whether it decisively refutes a drive-reduction theory or simply establishes the existence of a primary drive for physical contact is perhaps another matter.

A second implication of Freud's drive-reduction analysis is that in principle there need be no direct relationship between the mother's overt behavior and the infant's development of a bond to her. If bond formation is entirely a function of drive reduction and investment of attention and affect, then it is entirely the infant's point of view that matters. A mother's adequacy or inadequacy as a means of drive reduction can not easily be equated with the frequency, intensity, or patterning of specific maternal behaviors. Although this observation and the notion of an affective rather than a behavioral bond give rise to some of the most appealing and thoughtful psychoanalytic dissections of infant-mother or even adult-adult ties, they also combine to confound empirical analysis.

The Stability of the Infant-Mother Tie.   As mentioned above, Freud felt that the infant-mother tie was the strongest, the longest lasting, and the prototype of all later love relationships. This implies a distinction between love relationships and other types of relationships. Are peer relationships based on love? If not then the developmental significance that Freud had in mind for the infant-mother tie might have to be examined in very long-term studies that reached at least into adolescence or early adulthood.

The crucial implication here concerning stability depends on the meaning of the term *prototype*. What kind of stability or coherence across the life span did Freud intend? In the most literal sense the prototype notion could imply that an adult seeks a spouse who represents in some sense a symbolic recovery or substitute for a parental object. Alternatively the prototype notion might imply that the strength, quality, or patterning of an infant-adult relationship could provide a model or goal for subsequent relationships. Some literature on family disruptions and delinquency is consistent with this interpretation (e.g., Rutter, 1972). There may also be some relationship between early experience of family conflict and subsequent tendency toward spouse and child abuse (e.g. Rosenbaum & O'Leary, 1981). But it is not clear that these data require a psychodynamic interpretation. Finally, it is possible to interpret the notion of a prototype to imply only that infant-adult ties have all or many of the defining components of adult ties (e.g., affect, mutual support, channels of communication, responses to separation and loss). This implies that the infant-mother tie is a *structural* or *organizational prototype* of adult relationships and is in every sense truly a love relationship. Although this is the least restrictive interpretation of Freud's observation, it nonetheless would be a strong claim.

It is probably more useful simply to suggest these alternative interpretations than to wonder what Freud *really* meant. But perhaps we can speculate that the literal recovery of a parental figure may occasionally occur. The patterning of later relationships after relationships to parents (or perhaps in reaction against them) might occur somewhat more often. And it seems likely that the notion of a structural or organizational prototype is often, even usually, the case. The important point is that in the psychoanalytic view the infant-mother tie has significant implications for later development.

Behavioral and Social Learning Theories of Dependency

Nature of the Infant-Mother Tie.   In contrast to the strong emphasis of affect in psychoanalytic theories, behavioral and social learning theories have emphasized the observable aspects of the infant-mother bond. In particular, most have construed attachment/dependency relationships as strictly behavioral phenomena. In accordance with their strong commitment to operational definitions and objective measures, learning theorists have generally defined attachment behaviors as those that tend to increase and maintain infant-adult proximity. Gewirtz (1972a, 1972b) has broadly defined the class of relevant behaviors to include any that are contingent upon or are otherwise under the control of caretaker behavior. Affect is implicated only insofar as overt expressions, such as smiling and crying, meet these criteria.

This approach implies that attachment relationships differ primarily in strength and that the quantity of behavior emitted is a useful and by definition a valid index of onset and strength of the infant-adult bond. Attachment exists when the quantity of attachment behavior is greater than zero; increases in the frequency, duration, or intensity of attachment behavior imply a stronger bond; and characteristic declines in proximity seeking and separation protest from age 2 to age 4 imply attenuation of the bond.

In addition, most learning theory formulations imply that differences among attachment relationships and between attachment and other relationships are entirely matters of overt behavioral preference. No special status is accorded the infant's first attachment and except for differences in behavioral content few distinctions are made between infant or child-parent relationships, friendships among peers, and love relationships. Finally, learning theories pose no necessary limits on the number of figures toward whom attachment behavior might be directed.

The Origins of a Behavioral Bond.   One hallmark of behavioral learning theories is a consistent emphasis on external control. Whether by mechanisms of classical conditioning, explicit reinforcement, or consistent temporal association with caregiver behavior, the major determinants of proximity seeking and maintenance are assumed to be in the environment. This implies a clear relationship between parental behavior and the frequency/intensity of infant behavior. Attachment should not arise in the absence of parental behavior and should be strongest when parental input is greatest.

Because a very wide range of adult behaviors can be construed as potentially reinforcing, learning theorists have not emphasized any specific subset of behaviors that might be designated ''parental'' (as opposed to any other form of interactive behavior). Many different adult behaviors might control and elicit the same collection of infant responses.

The Stability of a Behavioral Bond.   Behavioral learning theories suggest a variety of mechanisms that might mediate a stable infant–adult bond. These could include the consistent availability and salience of one or a few adults and/or temporally stable patterns of reinforcement for approach and proximity maintenance. Indeed when marked clinging and separation protest occur in infancy, they can be strikingly stable across time and situations. However no postulate of any major learning theory implies or predicts that any aspect of the infant–adult bond is *necessarily* stable across time and context. In every case consistency is explained by reference to the environment, and great emphasis is placed on the situational specificity of behavior. There is very little emphasis on the infant as a determinant of its own behavior. Accordingly few implications of infant–adult bonds for later behavior or development arise in learning theory formulations. Whereas this position on the issue of stability contrasts sharply with the predictions of psychoanalytic theory, there is not yet a strong empirical basis upon which to decide the matter.

Ethological Attachment Theory

Nature of the Infant–Mother Bond.   Ethological attachment theory emphasizes first and foremost that patterns of infant–adult attachment are evolved species-specific behavioral adaptations. Presumably the primary adaptive advantage of maintaining infant–adult proximity is protection of the infant against predation. Having emphasized this, Bowlby (1969), Ainsworth (1972), Sroufe and Waters (1977) and others have defined important roles for affect and cognition as well as behavior in the organization and operation of attachment relationships. For example, it is evident that infant attachment behavior is highly sensitive to context and to the infant's state and evaluation of salient stimuli. This sensitivity depends on cognition. In addition the stimuli which seem to have the most consistent impact on attachment behavior (e.g., novel objects or environments and distance from the caregiver) also tend to elicit affective responses. Moreover the effects of these stimuli are most easily predicted when infant affective state is taken into account. Strange objects, dark places, and separation from watchful adults were probably correlated with risk of predation in the early environment to which the human infant is adapted. Thus many infant fears may have a biologically rational basis. Nonetheless the same stimuli can be enjoyed when the context is playful and an attachment figure is close at hand.

Ethological attachment theory places more emphasis on the function of maintaining proximity to adults and using them as a base from which to explore than it places on any particular behavior. Attachment is inferred from the organization of behavior across contexts and across time. It is never equated with a single behavior or with the quantity of behavioral output per se. Indeed performance of many behaviors that serve the attachment system (e.g., crying or clinging) at consistently high intensity would be antithetical to the adaptive function of the infant–adult bond. After all, the use of an adult as a secure base supports exploration and thus supports cognitive and social development as obviously as it supports survival.

Origins of the Infant–Adult Bond.   Ethological attachment theory assumes that attachment is learned. However one of its strongest postulates is that this learning is facilitated by species-specific biases in learning abilities; that is, the acquisition of typical patterns of attachment behavior is assumed to be easier and more likely (given the average expectable environment) than acquisition of an equally complex but randomly constituted set of behaviors. Hypothesizing a biological basis for attachment does not imply that it is innate. It simply suggests that the innate learning abilities of particular species provide a bias toward response to certain stimuli and toward the integration of skills that work together as components of the attachment system.

Neither drive reduction nor explicit reinforcement of specific behaviors play important roles in ethological attachment theory. The primary basis for acquisition of an infant–adult bond is assumed to be species-characteristic patterns of social interaction. In contrast to the view that any reinforcer should be able to establish attachment behaviors, this view implies that some parental inputs are more relevant than others to bond formation. An infant's experience of contingent adult responsiveness to signals and coordination of behavioral and affective response with adults may be primary among these. It may not be necessary for an adult ever to have comforted or protected an infant for it to seek comfort and protection in a moment of need. But this remains an empirical question.

Although ethological attachment theory assumes that attachment is learned, it equates attachment with a pattern of behavior across time, not with any specific response. Because, in this view, attachment does not occur within the kind of temporal context necessary for close operant analyses, other methods and levels of analyses seem better suited to the question, "What is learned in the formation of an infant–adult bond?" Consistent with this ethological theory implies that the amount of interaction necessary for attachment formation is loosely a function of the complexity of the behavior pattern to be learned. In humans at least this implies substantially more time than would be necessary to establish behavioral dependency via explicit reinforcement. Secure-base behavior in humans is not usually evident before 10 months. Separation protest occurs earlier.

Stability of the Infant–Adult Bond.   The notion of species-specific biases in learning implies a degree of similarity among attachment relationships across infants. It probably also implies a degree of buffering against moderate environmental variation. In addition the very complexity of the attachment behavioral system lends a certain inertia that might span temporary changes in the environment. Finally, the interactive nature of attachment behavior implies that an infant actively operates to maintain the social environment to which its behavior is adapted. Accordingly, in normal and reasonably stable environments, the use of an adult as a base from which to explore should be stable across time. As indicated later the empirical data support this expectation.

At the same time, ethological theory identifies attachment with maintenance of a degree of proximity across time and with the secure-base phenomenon, not with specific behaviors. Consequently, as the infant's behavioral repertoire and cognitive abilities change with development, the content and patterning of proximity and secure-base behavior will change. Visual and vocal interaction may suffice where physical contact was once required. The infant's excursions away from its caregiver eventually last longer and span wider distances. With increasing cognitive abilities the secure base becomes portable. Literal access to the parent becomes a broader confidence in parental support and perhaps eventually becomes confidence in one's own abilities. In any event, ethological attachment theory does not predict stability of behavioral detail across time or situations. It does predict coherence and consistency at the level of adaptive functioning vis-à-vis one or a few supportive adults.

Finally, ethological attachment theory per se implies very little about the relationship between infant–adult attachment and later social development. At the same time Bowlby and Ainsworth both have continuing interests in psychodynamic theories of personality and have suggested relationships to later behavior that are consistent with ethological theory but are not necessarily derived from it. Sroufe and Waters (1977) and others have also tried to incorporate ethological attachment theory into an integrative organismic psychology of social development and competence. This can be useful, but ethological attachment theory remains primarily a theory of the nature of infant–mother bonds. As such its value rests primarily on the comparative/evolutionary emphasis and the focus on behavioral adaptation that it introduces to the study of personality and social development. Its empirical implications, boundaries, and limitations are not easily defined.

MODELS OF THE INFANT–MOTHER BOND

Attachment and dependency are often interesting to view as differing in amount from one individual to another and from one age to the next during development. In other contexts it is more interesting or important to point out the complexity of organization among attachment behaviors and the relationship between attachment behavior and classes of environmental and cognitive/affective stimuli. In yet other contexts it is most important to emphasize that attachment involves two people, not just one, and that attachment relationships differ along many dimensions within and across dyads.

These perspectives are not uniquely associated with any particular theories of the infant-mother bond. Indeed it would not be advantageous for a theory to restrict its focus to only one perspective. They are more properly identified with *models* of what kind of construct attachment is to be. Whatever theoretical orientation one adopts, the traitlike consistencies of attachment phenomena, the organization of attachment behaviors along the lines of a distinct behavioral system, and the fact that attachment is a multifaceted relationship that exists across time all deserve close attention. Indeed a thorough description of the infant-mother bond requires description from each of these perspectives.

Unfortunately models of the infant-mother bond are often only implicitly adopted. They are not often well defined and alternatives are rarely explored systematically within a given theoretical framework. The outlines of trait, behavioral system, and relationship models are sketched in this section in order to clarify the distinction between theory and models and hopefully to facilitate systematic exploration in future discussions. More detailed reviews are presented by Wiggins (1973), Bischof (1975), Hinde (this volume) and a comparison of various models is provided by Waters (1980).

Trait Models

Trait models are the conventional vehicles of personality research and the study of individual differences. In essence a trait model assumes a single underlying basis or theme for a variety of related behaviors. These behaviors are assumed to be useful indices of the "strength" of a behavioral consistency or of an underlying cause. Because the behaviors index the same construct or have the same cause, they are usually assumed to be intercorrelated. This approach emphasizes the consistency of behavior across time and situations at the expense of attention to its organization or interpersonal aspects. Adopted strategically this emphasis can offer powerful conceptual and empirical leverage for the analyses of attachment phenomena. Adopted incidentally as an artifact of conventional assessment paradigms and left unstated, a trait approach can lead (and has often led) to unreasonable predictions about the consistency versus environmental responsiveness of behavior and about the contexts in which behavior occurs as well as its causes.

An implicit trait model is adopted whenever the "strength" of attachment or dependency is assessed in terms of the frequency or intensity of specific behaviors. Trait models or at least trait-type descriptions are also involved when an infant-adult attachment is characterized in qualitative categories such as secure or anxious.

For various purposes it may often be useful to summarize the consistency of attachment behavior by describing an infant as clingy or vocal or independent. Or it may be useful to describe one infant as generally seeming confident in its mother's availability and responsiveness and another infant as less so. Both types of description have proven useful in the past.

A problem arises however when such trait-descriptive language begins to imply that an attachment trait is the *cause* of the consistency. This is a step too far. But it is a step often taken because it is so bound up in the traditional methodology of personality assessment. As Wiggins (1974) emphasizes, consistency is worth summarizing and often affords a useful basis for prediction, but traits are "lost causes." They require rather than offer explanations.

Behavioral System Models

A relatively recent approach to the problem of organization and continuity in the context of flexible and changing behavior patterns is the analysis of "systems" underlying the structure of behavior (e.g., Miller, Galanter, & Pribram, 1960; Baehrends, 1975; Bertelanffy, 1969; Bischof, 1975). The study of behavioral systems attempts to describe the mechanisms that organize behavior and contribute both stability and flexibility to social behavior. It is an attempt to specify one aspect of the individual's contribution to interactive phenomena that are dyadic (if not even more complex) in nature. From a behavioral systems perspective every individual brings an internal structural basis for coordinating and regulating behavioral and affective response to any interactive situation. One great advantage of behavioral systems models over modified S–R and other linear models is their ability to take into account the effects of contextual variables that manifestly affect most social behavior. This is an important characteristic because the argument for situationalism in the study of behavior (Mischel, 1968, 1973) depends on the assumption that there are no models of behavioral consistency that can accomplish this. The development of models that can meet the situationalist challenge is one alternative to adopting situationalism by default rather than on its merits.

Characteristics of Behavioral Systems.[1]   The simplest model for a behavioral system is a thermostat, an apparatus for regulating the behavior of a heating plant. The basic elements of a self-regulating system are a *receptor* which accepts some type of environmental input (e.g., temperature data); a *center* which in some way reacts to the input; and an *effector,* which on signal from the center generates some response to the environmental input (e.g., switch burner off). The output of the control system is monitored by a *feedback loop* to the receptor, which thereby appraises the system of the effects of its response (e.g., "It's cooling off now"). Continuous monitoring of the environment and

---

[1]Sections of this discussion are adapted from Waters (1980).

reference to some standard ("set point" or "set goal") makes self-regulation possible. More complex systems can of course be imagined.

Models of this kind have found wide applicability in research on animal behavior as alternatives to teleological explanations and untenable drive models of motivated and apparently purposive behavior. Behavioral systems capture both the stability and the context sensitivity of behavior. At the same time they are easily integrated into developmental models. This is because in their more elaborate forms, behavioral systems share the following characteristics:

1. *Structure.*   In contrast to unitary drives behavioral systems have components. These include sensors, effectors, comparators, etc.

2. *Interreference.*   The components of a behavioral system receive input not only about the environment but about the status of other components within the system. Insofar as this input influences the action of a given component, one component of a behavioral system can be part of the "environment" of other components. This is a major feature contributing to the ability of behavioral systems to take situational or contextual information into account in responding to a stimulus. It affords the opportunity to make responses conditional upon contextual variables and plays an important role in the development and organization of adaptive behavior.

3. *Selectivity.*   Behavioral systems do not respond to every type of environmental stimulus or even to the entire range of stimuli from a single source. This is due in part to and is reflected in species-characteristic constraints and biases in learning abilities.

4. *Calibration.*   The "goal" of a behavioral system is specified by the values of internal parameters to which various inputs are compared. Homeostats have fixed values for these parameters. More complex designs may adjust the parameters in real time by reference to information about either internal or external events or states, as these bear upon the system's status relative to its environment.

5. *Integrity.*   The components of a behavioral system are organized such that the system acts as a whole; that is, a response to a stimulus is not the interaction of several components' responses; it is the single (perhaps complex) response selected after all relevant inputs from components are compiled. A behavioral system may often generate behavioral outputs that compete with the output of another system, but a given system is not conceived of as competing with itself to produce a response.

6. *Need for support.*   The behaviors initiated, modulated, or terminated by the effector components of a behavioral system are not properly part of the system. They belong to the animal's repertoire of action skills. Any action skill may at various times serve more than one behavioral system. In addition a behavioral system may require input from the operation of relevant action skills during development in order to become properly organized and calibrated.

7. *Development.*   Behavioral systems are not necessarily operative or even assembled at birth.

8. *Adaptation.*   The developmental blueprint for a given behavioral system reflects a species' long experience with an ''average expectable environment.'' In that context the system can provide relevant and adaptive responses to environmental inputs. In other contexts, either as a consequence of developmental deviations or of the type of inputs received, the system may not provide adaptive responses.

It may well be objected that models of this complexity violate the principle of parsimony. But it is important to remember that the principle of parsimony applies to the explanation of a phenomenon, not to its definition. Modified S–R models and causal trait models are only parsimonious explanations of infant-adult ties when we define these relationships in terms narrow enough to fit such models. Suppose instead that we first *describe* the behavioral bases of infant-adult ties in their own right and then search for parsimonious explanations; that is, suppose we allow that infant–adult ties exist in some substantive sense and that defining them to suit our models will not make them so. Suddenly, modified S–R and causal trait models appear inadequate or become complexly ad hoc and cumbersome. The elegance and simplicity of behavioral systems models is most apparent when the behavioral complexity and context sensitivity of infant–adult ties is recognized and understood in detail.

Bischof (1975) has presented an elaborate general systems formulation of the attachment–exploration balance and has incorporated the notion of ''felt security'' into his model. And although he sees it as only a small step toward conceptualizing behavior in systems terms, it is an elegant integration of current theories of attachment, fear, and exploration. The model also suggests interesting possibilities for incorporating individual differences parameters such as dependency and enterprise as codeterminants of the action of behavioral systems. In Fig. 2.1 we have proposed a simplification and extension of Bischof's model of attachment and exploratory systems and their interactions. We have retained Bischof's notation and whereas the model may seem complex at first glance, it is in fact much simpler than an infant. A closer approximation to a complete model would certainly be vastly more involved. Nonetheless the model proposed here can convey the sense of a behavioral systems approach to the attachment construct; it can help summarize the observations and predictions upon which (in this case) ethological-organizational attachment theory rests; and in emphasizing the context sensitivity and environmental responsiveness of attachment behavior it can vividly illustrate the limitations of simple trait models.

The symbols used in the model are as follows. Organisms and objects (e.g., primary attachment figure, nonsocial objects, infant) are enclosed by double lines. The larger system represents the infant and only its internal systems are

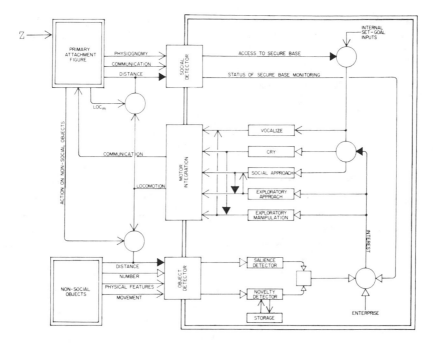

FIG. 2.1.   Simplified Model of an Attachment Behavioral System

presented. Blocks indicate systems or subsystems within the infant system. These may either involve sensory processing or motor programming. Variables within the infant system are indicated by arrows. The orientation of the arrowheads indicates direction of causation: Arrows pointing toward blocks (inputs) act on arrows leading from the same block (output variables). Arrows originating in open space (e.g., "internal set goal inputs") are influences not fully specified by the model but worthy of note. Arrows branch when a variable acts on more than one block. Open triangular arrowheads indicate that a variable is positively correlated with the output variables it influences. Solid triangular arrowheads indicate that a variable is negatively correlated with the output variables it influences. Two-line arrowheads indicate influences that can be either positive or negative and are not specified by the model. Small open circles represent an operation resembling addition (inputs are added [or subtracted] to determine influence on output). Small squares represent an operation resembling multiplication (if either input is zero, the value of output is zero). Note that only a few of the features of the primary attachment figure and of nonsocial objects that can influence the infant are indicated by arrows between these systems. The many external factors that can influence the primary attachment figure are represented by the single arrow, Z. Finally, within the infant system, arrows indicating motor outputs (more precisely outputs to action skills) are connected by arrows simply to reflect a few of the operations accomplished during motor integration that limit the value of single behaviors as indices of attachment.

The major differences between the present model and Bischof's involve the elimination of a complex array of motivational constructs and drives from the infant system, definition of causal arrows in terms more directly tied to ethological attachment theory than to psychodynamic motivational theories, and specification of motor output interactions. Of course it would also be possible to build models that emphasized motivation and affect and were less closely tied to behavior.

In brief the model specifies that the infant's attachment behaviors are complexly influenced in a coordinated manner by features of the social and nonsocial environment and by the structure of the attachment behavioral system. Within the infant system, exploratory behavior is influenced by characteristics of nonsocial objects, by an individual differences variable reflecting the consequences of past behavior (enterprise), and by the status of the secure-base monitor (essentially a function of time away from the adult and/or change in the location or behavior of the adult). Similarly, proximity-seeking behavior is influenced by the accessibility of the primary attachment figure, by internal set goal inputs such as infant state, recent events in the environment, and perhaps selected individual differences. In addition, proximity-seeking behavior is influenced by the degree of competing interest elicited by salient and novel objects in the environment.

In contrast to trait models, which equate all instances of similar behaviors, the model distinguishes two types of locomotion, social approach and exploratory approach. The latter can be directed toward nonsocial objects, unfamiliar social objects, and even toward attachment figures, especially during play and interaction that involves sharing objects. Thus approach per se is not invariably an index of attachment and approach to objects has different implications than approach to conspecifics. The model also specifies that related modes of motor response can be viewed as alternatives and that they need not be expected to show strong positive correlations, as required by trait models.

A much more complex model would be required to capture the actual complexity of the attachment–exploration balance, much less to capture the variety of behavior in interactive play between infant and adult. The model proposed here at least has the advantage of pointing to the types of data needed for extensions of this approach. In addition it defines the attachment–exploration phenomenon in a complexity that is closer to the behavioral details and at the same time apparently beyond the scope of the trait constructs that have dominated attachment theory for so long.

The major advantage of behavioral systems models is that they help summarize the breadth of the phenomenon to which the term *attachment* refers. In addition, they help summarize the complex of relationships, interactions, and responses that a specific theory implies. It should be possible to build models like the one presented above to illustrate psychodynamic theories and several types of learning-based theories of attachment. This could broaden the descriptive value of both. It could also clarify unstated differences between theorists and thus facilitate useful discussion.

Models of Attachment as a Relationship

Attachment always involves two people with a history of shared interactive contact over a period of time. Models of attachment as a relationship emphasize the interactive and dyadic aspects of infant–adult or adult–adult bonds. Where trait models emphasize one participant's perspective and summarize the consistencies in an individual's behavior, models of relationships take the dyad as the unit of analysis and focus upon both change and consistency in a sequence of interactions over time. Similarly, where behavioral systems models emphasize the contemporaneous determinants of behavior, models of relationships place strong emphasis on the fact that the determinants of ongoing interactions include previous interactions. This implies that major determinants of current behavior lie in the past, even in the relatively distant past. Relationship models emphasize that this may be particularly the case within dyads that interact consistently rather than intermittently or infrequently, that is, in ongoing relationships. In a word, relationships provide a context in which dyadic behavior occurs; the use of relationship models emphasizes the contextual (as opposed to individual or situational) determinants of behavior.

The study of infant–adult bonds as relationships is a very recent development (e.g., Hinde, 1976a, 1976b, and the present volume). And so far the approach remains more descriptive than analytical. Nonetheless relationship models deserve considerable attention because this approach and level of analysis is yielding descriptive insights that would not have arisen from the quantitative trait paradigm or the formalisms of systems models.

Describing Relationships.[2]   To describe relationships it is necessary to describe both the content and quality of interactions that occur. It is also necessary to describe how interactive behaviors are patterned, their absolute frequencies, relative frequencies, when they occur with respect to each other, and how they affect each other. Ultimately we make an abstraction in characterizing a relationship from observations of interactions.

Hinde (1976a) has suggested eight dimensions along which relationships can be said to differ: (1) content of component interactions; (2) diversity of interactions; (3) reciprocity versus complementarity; (4) qualities of component interactions; (5) relative frequency and patterning of interactions; (6) multidimensional qualities (e.g., "warmth," "rejectingness"); (7) levels of perspective; and (8)

---

[2]Sections of this discussion are adapted from Waters (1980).

penetration. Several of these deserve at least a brief explanation. There are undoubtedly more dimensions that could be added to the list.

Content of Interactions.   The quality of any relationship may depend on the presence or prominence of certain types of interactions. Infant–mother attachment relationships certainly entail many different kinds of interactions that are never observed in the laboratory or that cannot be captured in terms of discrete behavioral acts (e.g., categories of interactive behavior such as play, affection, punishment). We can use the content of interactions to distinguish among types of relationships (e.g., friendship vs. love) as well as to distinguish between different relationships of the same type. For example, we are more likely to describe a relationship as harmonious if there is a predominance of positive affect in interaction and if interactions are initiated and concluded without conflict than if negative affect and conflict predominate. Brief observations are not well suited to this type of data, nor are observations in only one or a few contexts or occasions.

Diversity of Interactions.   Some infant–mother relationships are largely characterized by routine caretaking whereas others appear to have more breadth, a wider range of interactive patterns. Some mothers may *see* their interactions with their infant in terms of a few types of interaction, and others view the same behaviors in more highly differentiated terms. One feels trapped by the routine; the other finds it anything but routine. All relationships change in the diversity of interactions across time, a fact not reflected in the analyses of Strange Situation behavior. Hinde (1976a, pp. 5–6) discusses several reasons for the diversification of interactive behaviors within a relationship.

Reciprocity versus Complementarity.   Infant–adult interactions are dyadic affairs; that is they are better viewed in terms of the role each partner plays in the behavior of the other than in terms of the behavior of each taken alone. When both participants in an interaction show similar behavior patterns, the interaction is said to be reciprocal in nature. When the interaction is carried out by the meshing of different repertoires of behavior, the relationship is said to be complementary. Infant–adult interactions are, by nature, complementary in the beginning. But dyads differ in the extent to which complementarity is developed. Insofar as a mother allows and facilitates her infant's participation in interaction she is laying the foundation for the later development of reciprocity, in what Bowlby (1969) called a ''goal-corrected partnership.'' Ainsworth has spoken of this aspect of interaction in terms of the mother's cooperation versus interference with the infant's ongoing behavior (Ainsworth, Bell, & Stayton, 1971). Hinde proposes that complementarity and reciprocity in interactions and the extent to which interaction is codetermined or unilaterally dictated are important determinants of both stability and change in relationships.

Qualities of interactions.   One important quality of interactions within relationships is the extent to which the behavior of one partner is coordiated with or "meshes" with the behavior of the other. Ainsworth has discussed maternal sensitivity to infant signals in just these terms (Ainsworth et al., 1971). Sensitivity involves: (1) perceiving the signal; (2) correctly interpreting it; (3) selecting an appropriate response; and (4) delivering the response in a timely (or contingent) fashion. A given maternal behavor in response to a signal may be timely and appropriate, or it may be inappropriate or too delayed for the infant to notice the contingency. Sensitivity or contingent responsiveness may be characteristic of a wide diversity of interactions or limited to one or a few domains (e.g., play but not feeding or other caretaking situations). There are, of course, many more qualities of infant–mother interactions that could be mentioned. Because the rewards obtained in a relationship may depend not only on what the participants do together but also on how they do it, Hinde suggests that qualities of interactions may be of crucial importance for the stability of relationships.

Relative Frequency and Patterning of Interactions.   We are not always interested only in the absolute frequency of different behaviors or types of interaction. For example, the relative rather than absolute frequency of maternal behaviors is the key characterizing interactions as responsive or unresponsive. In addition, certain emergent qualities of interactions (e.g., consistency) are not characteristic of any one interaction but only of the patterning of interactions across time.

Multidimensional Qualities.   Many qualities of interactions cannot be identified with the presence/absence or intensity of a given behavior, but depend instead on the concurrence of a number of characteristics. Many everyday judgments about relationships turn out to depend on such multidimensional observations. For example, Hinde suggests that we are most likely to describe a relationship as an affectionate relationship (or bond) if:

1. It involves a diversity of interactions.
2. It is of long duration.
3. Both partners act to regain proximity when separated from one another.
4. The behavior of each is organized in relation to the ongoing behavior of the other.
5. The presence of the partner alleviates distress due to strange objects or situations.
6. Actions conducive to the welfare of the other are likely to be repeated.

Not all of these imply bonding or attachment nor is each always present in such relationships. This characterization points, among other things, to the weakness of unidimensional characterizations of relationships (as in "strength") and to the inherent weakness of simple operational definitions of multidimensional phenomena. It also makes clear that such qualities will be hard to assess from brief observations of a few behaviors in only a few contexts on only a few occasions.

Penetration.   The development of an attachment relationship begins with familiarity and goes to intimacy. Characteristics such as the breadth of interaction, uniqueness of interaction, sensitivity and accuracy of communication, pacing of interaction (meshing), degree of spontaneity, and selectivity of responsiveness are involved in the degree of penetration we attribute to a relationship. Relationships differ in the extent to which they constitute an individual's social experience and in their salience on the social landscape. At first an infant would seem incapable of experiencing a relationship of great penetrance. With the onset of attachment we generally consider that there is almost exclusive investment in one or a few figures. As peers become more salient, the child–mother tie is often said to diminish. But it seems more accurate to say that the penetrance of the relationship diminishes; although a child's horizons broaden, his love may last. The penetrance of a relationship with an infant will differ from adult to adult, and across time as well.

Theories and Models

The theories and models outlined here suggest a two-way classification for future approaches to the infant–mother bond. No doubt there is a proverbial kernal of truth to each of the theories we have presented. Moreover each of the models discussed appears to have advantages as a mode of conceptualizing the infant–mother bond. In the past, however, theorists have not distinguished theoretical perspective from the selection of models. Ethological attachment theory is closely identified with behavioral system models and yet embraces notions of secure versus anxious attachment, which are clearly trait-type descriptions. Learning theories generally allow little room for trait concepts or even for the study of individual differences, and yet the learning analysis of dependency clearly assumes a quantitative trait-type construct. Psychoanalytic theory implies a systems model based on the organization and interaction of drive and energy concepts. At the same time psychoanalysts seem comfortable with trait language, even when referring explicitly to relationships.

In principle each of the theories summarized here could be explored using each of the models described as a tool to examine and emphasize different aspects of the infant–mother bond. If this could be accomplished, the descriptive and empirical foundations of each theory could be broadened. This could only improve the prospects for discussions and integration across the boundaries of theoretical perspective. More importantly, systematic mapping of theories into various models could help us understand attachment phenomena in their own right. The alternative is to continue letting theorists define the infant–adult bond to suit the needs of theory.

CRITIQUES OF THE ATTACHMENT CONSTRUCT

Recent theory and research have tended to focus on infant–adult interaction per se and to avoid defining or assessing emergent outcomes such as an infant–mother bond of attachment. To some extent this is useful. Interactive behavior in infancy involves cognitive and behavioral skills that are often underestimated in formal test-type observations. In addition, if attachment arises from interaction, then detailed knowledge of early interactions should help answer the question, "What is learned in the formation of an infant–adult bond?" It can be useful therefore to define and study interactive phenomena in their own right and to afford this line of study some independence from the conventions of attachment theory and research.

Movement toward the study of interaction does not have to involve a move away from the infant–mother bond or the attachment construct. Nonetheless critics have recently argued that the notion of an infant–adult bond has not been well defined and may in some sense defy definition (e.g., Weinraub, Brooks, & Lewis, 1977). Others have pointed to the problems that arise in translating attachment theory into meaningful measurements (e.g., Cohen, 1974; Weinraub et al., 1977). Rosenthal (1973) has even suggested that everything implied by the notion of a "bond" between infant and adult can be captured in the sequential details of interactive behavior. For her there is no attachment, only interaction. Most of this criticism or, if you like, discouragement, arises from problems mentioned above. Theories are advanced with many unstated postulates and implications; the same language is used to refer to fundamentally different phenomena; different facets of the same phenomenon are often construed as competitors; and there is a tendency to accept a trait model uncritically and without also exploiting useful alternatives.

The critiques cited above raise conceptual issues that we think will be clarified and resolved. In some cases clarification itself will resolve an issue. In other cases clarification of theory and explicit definitions of models will at least facilitate debate and stimulate discriminating research. But this will not be enough. Conceptual critiques are at least implicitly founded upon a perception of empirical failure or stagnation. This perception deserves careful attention.

A Recent Empirical Critique

Personality psychologists have developed a number of strategies for assessing the validity of hypothetical constructs. These involve careful integration of theory and data and usually involve data from a variety of sources (Cronbach & Meehl,

1955). Construct validation is necessary whenever we are unwilling to adopt a strict operational definition of a variable (e.g., to equate attachment with one or a few specific behaviors). In general constructs are validated by confirmation of predicted associations among variables.

Because most personality variables have been conceptualized as traits, these have received the most careful attention in the literature on construct validation. As outlined by Campbell and Fiske (1959), the essence of trait construct validation involves establishing that a trait measure is reliable (i.e., it yields reproducible scores) and has both convergent and discriminant validity. A trait measure has convergent validity if it correlates with other measures predicted by theory. It has discriminant validity if it is uncorrelated with theoretically unrelated variables.

Applying these criteria to the correlational data on infant–mother attachment, Masters and Wellman (1974) concluded that there is little empirical support for an attachment construct in the existing literature. In particular they found that when attachment is measured in terms of discrete behaviors (looking at, vocalizing to, approaching, touching, crying during separation) it is difficult to obtain reproducible correlational results within or across samples. In addition scores on these behaviors during brief laboratory observations tend to be unstable over periods ranging from 6 months to as few as 3 minutes. In addition, there was little evidence that these presumed indices of attachment were substantially intercorrelated. Masters and Wellman found few data from which to assess discriminant validity, but lacking positive evidence for either stability or convergent validity, the negative implications seemed clear enough. Masters and Wellman concluded that meaningful assessments of individual infants with respect to attachment were not supported, and they proposed that future research emphasize the situational determinants of interactive behavior, proximity seeking, and separation protest.

Masters and Wellman's (1974) critique is modeled upon Mischel's (1968) situationist critique of personality research in general and individual differences research in particular. Unfortunately, by adopting the Campbell and Fiske (1959) methodology, Masters and Wellman tacitly adopted the view that the infant–adult bond can only be conceptualized as a quantitative trait construct. If this had been made explicit, it would have been more apparent that their review afforded, at most, a critique of research on attachment as a causal trait. As it is, their review has tended to discourage interest in the study of attachment from any perspective.

Negative Evidence

Negative evidence can bear many interpretations. According to Cronbach and Meehl (1955), negative evidence in construct validation research can arise from three conditions: (1) failure to measure the construct well; (2) successful measurement but failure to test a reasonable deduction from the theory of the construct (or use of an experimental design that is itself flawed); or (3) successful measurement and decisive failure to confirm a reasonable prediction. Conditions (1) and (2) do not allow any negative conclusions concerning construct validity. Only (3) is valid negative evidence and it can be adopted only when (1) and (2) have been ruled out. Only (3) is seriously entertained in Masters and Wellman's critique. The data reviewed below examine the possibility of measurement failures in studies of infant–mother attachment. In addition our own program of research is summarized as an indication that with effective measurement derived from ethological theory and both behavioral systems and relationship models, more encouraging results can be obtained. In particular substantial stability across time and many theoretically relevant correlates of qualitative individual differences in attachment can be demonstrated.

Assessing Attachment

Over a decade ago, Ainsworth and Witting (1969) developed a standardized laboratory procedure during which infant attachment behavior is observed in an unfamiliar room and then heightened by a series of separations (mother leaves room) and reunions (mother returns). This procedure, the Strange Situation, has provided extensive data about the balance between attachment and exploratory behavior and about the eliciting and terminating conditions for attachment behavior. These data primarily involve group means on various behaviors across the eight 3-minute episodes of the Strange Situation (i.e., they involve normative not individual differences data). This work is summarized in a recent review by Ainsworth, Blehar, Waters, and Wall (1978).

Unfortunately the Strange Situation has become, by convention, *the* attachment situation. The vast majority of attachment assessments have involved this or related procedures and the assumption that one infant's behavior here is representative of behavior at home or in other contexts is rarely confirmed by concurrent observations. Moreover, it is often assumed that because this is *the* attachment situation, any behavior observed here is related to or can serve as a measure of attachment, as if temperament, cognitive level, infant state, and maternal behavior were somehow neutralized. The important point here is that a procedure that affords good normative data does not necessarily afford useful individual differences data. In addition no situation is so discriminating that only one variable can influence behavior in it. Discrimination has to be accomplished by careful definition of behavior categories. Given the same observation setting, some measures will be more valid than others vis-à-vis a particular construct. So it is with measures of attachment in the Strange Situation.

Most of the data reviewed by Masters and Wellman (1974) involved frequency counts or time samples of specific behaviors (touching, looking, vocalizing, crying) during episodes of 3–5 minutes in duration. In order for assessments of individuals to be useful, it is necessary to collect enough data to estimate an individual's typical behavior accurately. Brief observations can be very misleading, particularly if the behaviors scored are relatively rare in the first place. Measurements based on too little data tend to be subject to error or "noise," which makes them unreliable. Unreliable measurements are not reproducible (the same subject tends to receive different scores on repeated tests); they cannot reveal stability across time even if it is present; and they cannot correlate with measures of other variables (even if these are assessed more reliably).

In the research reviewed by Masters and Wellman, the behaviors scored did in fact occur at very low rates. Many occurred less than 1.5 times per minute in brief observation episodes. This means, among other things, that the range of individual differences observed was relatively restricted. This alone would limit the magnitude of correlations across time and across behaviors. In addition it raises the possibility that the observations upon which Masters and Wellman's critique rests were simply *too brief* to provide good estimates of an individual's mean rate of response. When a behavior occurs only rarely, a large number of observations are necessary to obtain reliable estimates of individual scores. Samples of 2, 3, or 5 instances of a behavior during one observation can easily fluctuate by 20–200% on the basis of differences in behavior that are very small. Is a child who looks at mother once today and twice tomorrow *twice* as attached in only one day's time?

One approach to this problem is afforded by the psychometric theory of test reliability (Magnusson, 1966; Nunnally, 1978). Procedures developed for assessing the reliability of psychometric tests can be applied to time-sampled behavioral data as well, and the proportion of error variance in a set of data can be expressed as: 1 − coefficient of reliability. In the present case the appropriate reliability index is Cronbach's *alpha* (Cronbach, 1951).

In a recent study Waters (1978) computed the reliability of data comparable to those reported by Coates, Anderson, and Hartup (1972a, 1972b) and reviewed by Masters and Wellman (1974). In a sample of 30 infants seen at 12 and 18 months of age, the median reliabilities of looking, vocalizing, smiling, gesturing, approaching, and touching the mother during 3-minute observation periods prior to and after separation were .30, .45, .39, and .43, respectively. In addition to affording a means of assessing reliability, psychometric theory also allows us to estimate the number of test items (or the duration of observation) necessary to achieve any desired level of reliability. Using the Spearman–Brown formula for this purpose, Waters (1978) estimated that from 20 to over 1000 minutes of observation would be necessary to achieve reliabilities of .90 for these assessments. Obviously the Strange Situation procedure cannot simply be extended to accommodate this duration of time sampling. Other settings have to be used or other ways of assessing behavior in the Strange Situation are needed.

These results indicate that the low stability and weak convergent validity of attachment measures cited by Masters and Wellman (1974) are not valid evidence against even a trait model of attachment. Nor are they a basis for discouragement with the attachment construct or the notion of an infant–adult bond. They are, if anything, an indictment of research in which paradigm and convention have displaced theory and common sense.

Assessment Alternatives.   Ainsworth and her colleagues have developed alternative approaches for assessing individual differences in the Strange Situation. Working from an ethological/behavioral systems perspective, they have emphasized the function of attachment behavior and have defined broad behavior categories that encompass a variety of behaviors that have the same consequences or predictable outcomes. Proximity seeking, contact maintaining, interaction over a distance, proximity and interaction avoiding, and resistance to contact are the major categories. These are scored on 7-point scales in each episode of the Strange Situation. Both Connell (1976) and Waters (1978) have found that this scoring is substantially more stable across a period of 6 months than frequency counts of discrete behaviors. This is especially true of behavior toward the mother in reunion episodes, where the correlations are in the range of .50–.70. In addition Ainsworth et al. (1978) have reported a wide range of non–Strange Situation correlates of these measures. They include a wide range of infant and maternal behaviors at home from as early as the first quarter of the first year of life.

In addition to these behavior categories, Ainsworth and her colleagues have defined profiles based on combinations of behavior categories. These highlight the importance of behavior toward the mother after reunion as an important index of the infant's ability to use her as a secure base from which to explore in the home. In brief, most one-year-old infants (about 70%) show strong proximity seeking and contact maintaining during reunion. They are easily comforted by contact and interaction and are able to return to play without continued distress. In addition this normative group of infants shows little if any negative behavior (anger, refusal to greet or interact, active resistance to contact even while crying) during reunion. These infants are designated securely attached because at home they use the mother effectively as a secure base from which to explore and appear confident in her availability and responsiveness. Two smaller groups (20% and 10%, respectively) tend to show either active avoidance of the mother upon reunion or to mix separation protest, proximity seeking, and active resistance to contact in a surprisingly ineffective and disorganized way. Both the avoidant and the resistant infants have difficulty using the mother as a secure base at home (Ainsworth, et al., 1971). Accordingly they are designated anxiously attached. Both Connell (1976) and Waters (1978) have reported that secure, anxious/avoidant, anxious/resistant classifications are highly stable in middle-class families across the interval from 12–18 months of age. Both studies employed large samples and approximately 90% of the infants in each study received the same classification at both ages. In addition, Ainsworth et al. (1978) have reported a wide range of correlates of these assessments from as early as the neonatal period to as late as age 3½ in the preschool play group. Some of these are reviewed in the following section. For our present purposes, the important point is that discouragement with the attachment construct is not well founded either in conceptual critiques or in empirical data.

Validation of the Attachment Construct: Recent Data

Validation of the attachment construct involves more than demonstrating stability or correlations among attachment measures. It is necessary to test and confirm a wide range of predictions concerning infant–mother interaction and attachment formation, attachment and exploratory behavior, relationships between attachment to a primary caretaker and formation of additional attachments, and the roles that attachment may play in later social development in the peer group. As new hypotheses are generated and tested, attachment theory is revised and elaborated. We come to understand the infant–mother bond more fully and at the same time gain confidence in both the theory and the data we are working with. The results described below are part and parcel of this process.

Neonatal Antecedents.   If attachment assessments are reliable and valid, they should not only correlate with themselves across time, they should have a wide range of relevant correlates. If attachment arises from interaction, then individual differences in infant–mother interaction should lead to differences among attachment relationships by the end of the first year. Because interaction is determined by the contributions of each partner in a process of mutual influence, it can be predicted that some aspects of early infant behavior might influence interaction and eventually be associated with outcomes of the attachment process.

Using Ainsworth's anxious/avoidant (Group A), secure (Group B), anxious/resistant (Group C) assessment technique, Waters, Vaughn, and Egeland (1980) have recently shown *that infant characteristics assessed during the first week after birth can be related to individual differences in attachment by age 1 year.* As indicated in Table 2.1, infants who were later classified as secure or even anxious/avoidant were very successful in meeting the challenges of neonatal adaptation as assessed by the Brazelton Neonatal Behavioral Assessment Scale. However infants later classified as anxious/resistant had difficulty during this period. As a consequence, they were less successful in tests of orienting toward objects and persons in the environment, their motor development was slow and their muscle tone was weak, and some of them had difficulty in physiological regulation. All of these have obvious relevance to the infant's potential as a partner in social interaction. Although all of the infants tested were healthy and eventually met the demands of neonatal adaptation, Waters et al. suggested that transient symptoms reflected difficulties in adaptive mechanisms that continue to influence interaction throughout the first year.

TABLE 2.1
Neonatal Behavior and Infant-Mother Attachment at Age One-Year

	Attachment Classification				
	Avoidant (A) (N = 24)	Secure (B) (N = 50)	Resistant (C) (N = 26)	C_1 (N = 11)	C_2 (N = 15)
Habituation:					
1. Response decrement to light (>5)	7.5	8.3	7.8	8.0	7.7*
2. Response decrement to rattle (>5)	6.8	7.3	6.9	7.2−	6.7
3. Response decrement to bell (>4)	8.0	7.6	7.3	6.5	7.8
4. Response decrement to pinprick (>3)	4.0	4.4	4.1	4.5	3.8
Orientation:					
5. Inanimate visual (red ball) (>5)	6.6	7.0	6.2*	5.8**	6.5
6. Inanimate auditory (rattle) (>6)	7.1	7.4	7.0	6.6*	7.3
7. Animate visual (face) (>4)	6.3	6.3	5.4*	4.9**	5.6
8. Animate auditory (voice) (>5)	7.6	7.7	7.2*	7.3	7.1
9. Animate visual and auditory (face and voice) (>4)	7.0	6.9	6.5	5.9**	7.0
10. Alertness (>4)	4.7	4.9	4.2*	3.3**	4.8
Motor maturity:					
11. General tonus (>3<8)	5.7	5.7	5.3**	5.5	5.2**
12. Motor maturity (>2)	4.1	4.3	4.3	3.4*	5.0
13. Pull to sit (>2)	4.8	5.3	4.5**	4.4*	4.7*
14. Cuddliness (body molding) (>2)	4.3	4.6	4.3	4.0*	4.5
15. Defense movement (>3)	7.1	7.0	6.9	6.8	7.0
State control:					
16. Consolability (>4)	6.5	5.6	4.9	5.3	4.6
17. Peak of excitement (>3<7)	5.1	5.6	5.9	5.9	5.9
18. Rapidity of buildup (<8)	2.9	3.0	3.4	4.1*	3.0
19. Lability of states (>3)	2.0	1.9	2.1	2.2	2.0
20. Self-quieting activity (>3)	5.0	5.1	4.7	4.6	4.8
21. Hand-to-mouth facility (>2)	6.3	6.5	6.0	5.9	6.1
Regulatory maturity:					
22. Irritability (<6)	3.6	3.8	4.3	5.0*	3.8
23. Activity (>2<8)	5.0	5.0	4.9	4.9	4.9

(*continued*)

TABLE 2.1—*Continued*

	Attachment Classification				
	Avoidant (A) (N = 24)	*Secure* (B) (N = 50)	*Resistant* (C) (N = 26)	C_1 (N = 11)	C_2 (N = 15)
24. Tremulousness (<6)	4.2	4.0	4.7	5.7**	3.9
25. Startle response (<4)	2.2	2.2	2.5*	2.8**	2.3
26. Lability of skin color (<6)	4.3	4.6	4.8	5.3	4.5
Reflexes:					
27. Number of deviant reflexes (<2)	.8	.7	1.0	1.1	.9

Note: Items 1–26 are scored on a scale of 1–9. The range of optimal scores is indicated in paren-
theses after each item.
*C group or subgroups differ from B group at .05 level.
**C group or subgroups differ from B groups at .025 level.

Early Maternal Behavior.   In a study of 26 infants at home during the first
year, Ainsworth et al. (1978) assessed a wide range of early maternal behaviors
that predicted to later patterns of infant attachment. As indicated in Table 2.2,
mothers of infants later classified anxiously attached were less responsive to
infant cries, less successful and to some extent averse to holding and bodily
contact, less successful in pacing face-to-face interaction and more matter of fact
in these encounters, and had more difficulty coordinating their behavior with the
infant's during feeding.

In contrast to the neonatal data, these show a variety of differences between
the infants later classified anxious/avoidant and anxious/resistant and the infants
classified secure. The difficulties of mothers whose infants were later classified
anxious/resistant articulate well with the picture of their infants presented in the
neonatal data. Their apparent unresponsiveness to crying and ineptness in physical contact and feeding could well arise from the fact that their infants' behavior
was not well organized; that is, it may be difficult to teach interactive behaviors
to these infants, and it may also be difficult for a mother to learn from them. The
lack of neonatal antecedents to the difficult interactions with infants later
classified anxious/avoidant may point to maternal attitudes and perhaps also to
environmental pressures on these mothers as early determinants of their interactive behavior. They appear more averse to physical contact or less effective in
face-to-face interaction than mothers of infants later classified anxious/resistant.
In addition, by the end of the first year, mothers of both avoidant and resistant
infants are rated less sensitive to infant signals, more prone to interference with
ongoing infant behavior, and less accessible than mothers of securely attached
infants. However the mothers of anxious avoidant infants are scored as more

TABLE 2.2
Behavior Displayed at Home by Mothers
of Infants in the Three Strange-Situation Classifactory Groups
(Mean Scores for the First Quarter)

Maternal Behavior	Avoidant (Group A)	Secure (Group B)	Resistant (Group C)	Significance of Difference Between B and Non-B
Responsiveness to Infant Crying				
Ignoring of crying	3.08	1.60	1.59	n.s.
Unresponsiveness to crying				
(minutes per hour)	6.77	3.64	9.35	.01
Behavior Relevant to Close Bodily Contact				
Mean Duration of a pick-up				
episode (in minutes)	5.20	8.70	7.80	.10
% of pick-ups in which M				
behaves affectionately	6.50	16.90	8.75	.05
% of holding time in which M				
is tender, careful	22.00	55.00	2.25	.001
% of holding time in which M				
is inept	28.00	5.00	41.00	.001
Aversion to physical contact	7.30	2.28	1.73	.01
Provides B with unpleasant				
experience	5.68	1.45	2.90	.005
Behavior Relevant to Face-to-Face Interaction				
Contingent pacing	20.70	52.90	10.90	.01
Silent, unsmiling initiation	28.70	12.20	11.30	n.s.
Routine manner	29.70	11.00	25.50	.01
Behavior Relevant to Feeding				
Timing of initiation	2.75	6.40	2.38	.001
Timing of termination	3.17	6.54	2.83	.001
Dealing with baby's food				
preferences	3.87	6.70	3.83	.01
Pacing according to baby's				
rate of intake	3.43	6.85	3.33	.01

rejecting of the infant's needs and desires than the mothers of either anxious/ resistant or secure infants (Ainsworth et al., 1978, p. 145). Notwithstanding these differences, it is useless to assess responsibility when relationships go awry. Whether mother or infant takes the first step, the other's behavior responds and eventually makes its own contribution to the deterioration of the relationship.

Infant Behavior at Age 1 Year. The relationships between neonatal behavior, early maternal behavior, and attachment classifications support both the reliability and validity of the classification scheme and the usefulness and coherence of the attachment construct. Nonetheless, it is important to establish that laboratory-based attachment classifications have a range of correlates in concurrent home behavior. As discussed previously, many of the discrete behaviors assessed in the Strange Situation are interesting in a normative perspective but are less interesting in studies of individual differences. When the task is to characterize particular relationships, particularly to describe the infant's ability to use the mother as a secure base, Strange Situation behaviors per se are of little interest. They are primarily of interest for the range of relevant nonlaboratory behaviors that they allow us to predict economically. If there were no relationship between laboratory behaviors and the secure-base phenomenon at home, we would not conclude that attachment cannot be assessed. We would simply have

TABLE 2.3
Measures of Behavior Displayed at Home by Infants
in the Three Strange-Situation Classificatory Groups
(Mean Scores for the Fourth Quarter)

	Avoidant	*Secure*	*Resistant*
Behavior at Home	$N = 6$	$N = 13$	$N = 4$
Crying and Communication			
Frequency of crying (episodes per hour)	4.70	3.74	4.18
Duration of crying (minutes per hour)	5.60[b]	3.03	8.07[b]
Communication	1.83	2.63	1.25[a]
Responses to Mother's Comings and Goings			
Crying when M leaves the room	20.33[b]	14.08	29.00[b]
Following when M leaves room	56.33	55.62	21.25[b]
Positive greeting when M enters	28.17[a]	39.08	23.00[a]
Crying and mixed greeting	12.33	9.46	17.25[b]
Behavior Relevant to Contact			
I. Responses to being picked up and held			
Positive response to being held	14.33[b]	40.00	20.75[a]
Negative response to being held	21.17[b]	6.15	23.00
II. Responses to being put down			
Positive response to being put down	59.83	68.69	50.25[b]
Negative response to being put down	39.17[b]	27.31	30.75[b]
III. Initiation and termination			
Initiation of pick-up	16.17	22.08	9.50[a]
Initiation of put-down	3.50	2.46	6.75
IV. Special forms of contact behavior			
Tentative contact behaviors	.76	.28	.19
Sinking in	.02[b]	.25	.20
Active contact behaviors	.02[a]	.40	.12
Compliance and Anger			
Compliance to mother's commands	54.00[b]	81.15	44.00[b]
Anger	7.83[c]	3.00	5.75[b]

[a] $p < .05$.
[b] $p < .01$.
[c] $p < .001$.

to undertake the difficult task of evaluating attachment and secure-base behavior in home and other ecological settings.

As mentioned previously, Ainsworth et al. (1971) have in fact demonstrated that classifications based on laboratory observations are strongly related to patterns of secure-base behavior at home at age 1 year. In addition, as indicated in Table 2.3, these laboratory assessments are related to a variety of specific behaviors that reflect the infant's ability to use the mother as a secure base and its ability to shift from attachment to exploratory and back easily and without disruption. This is especially evident in the difficulties that both anxious attachment groups have in being comforted by proximity and contact with the mother. These results are important because they clarify the nature of individual differences that result from various patterns of infant–mother interaction. These differences are often left unspecified when we refer to differences in "attachment." It is easier to avoid unintended trait concepts and reference to attachment as an entity within the infant when these behavioral referents of the anxious attachment concept are identified. In addition, it is easier to see how patterns of attachment at age 1 year could be related to later social development when we specify the behaviors through which these effects could be mediated.

Stability of Attachment and Environmental Stress.   A great deal has been made of the stability or lack of stability of attachment relationships. Critics have often implied that if attachment assessments are not stable they are necessarily unreliable and cannot be valid. But most theories of the infant–mother bond emphasize that attachments, like any other affectional relationship, continue to develop even after an affective bond is formed and they are responsive to changes in the behavior of either partner. If stresses in the environment impacted decisively upon maternal behavior, for example, over a period of time and yet assessments of infant attachment remained highly stable, this would seem to challenge rather than confirm the attachment construct as it is usually construed.

In a recent study, Vaughn, Egeland, Sroufe, and Waters (1979) assessed infant attachment relationships at 12 and 18 months in a sample of low socioeconomic-status families. In addition they asked the mothers to complete surveys concerning stressful events that had occurred between the 12 and 18 month assessments. The events surveyed included work, family and neighbors, finances, violence, involvement with the law, and health. In general, mothers of anxiously attached 18-month-olds reported significantly more stressful events for the 12–18-month period than mothers of secure infants. In addition attachment classifications were significantly stable across the 12–18-month period, though much less so than in more stable middle-class family environments. More importantly, as indicated in Table 2.4, the stressful events data were clearly related to patterns of stability and change. The lowest stress scores were associated with secure 12-month relationships that were also secure at 18 months. Intermediate scores were associated with anxious relationships that improved and with stable

TABLE 2.4
Maternal Report of Stressful Events
by Quality and Stability
of Infant-Mother Attachment

Attachment Classification		Stressful-Events Score	
12 months	18 months	$\bar{X}$	SD
Secure	Anxious (10). . . .	10.00	3.27
Anxious	Anxious (24). . . .	6.83	2.93
Anxious	Secure (21).	6.04	4.47
Secure	Secure (45).	4.87	3.09

Note: N in parentheses.

anxious relationships. The highest stress scores were found in families in which a secure relationship had changed to anxious at 18 months. These results reflect the environmental responsiveness of interactive behavior and attachment in infancy. The notion of attachment as a relationship can comprehend both the stability data reported by Waters (1978) and Connell (1976) and the present data on change; the notion of attachment as a causal trait or dependency as a temperament variable cannot.

Attachment and Later Social Competence. As described earlier, both psychoanalysts and ethological/organismic theorists hypothesize that the infant–mother bond has important implications for later social development. In addition social learning theorists have often supposed that some aspects of attachment behavior might generalize to peers and at least support early patterns of friendship and play. From an evolutionary/adaptational point of view, it is arguable that patterns of attachment should articulate well with subsequent social development and at least afford some easy transition to wider social contacts. Because attachment and the development of peer relations are presumably adapted to the same long-term outcome, they should be well adapted to each other.

Waters, Wippman, & Sroufe (1979) have recently reported a longitudinal study of 32 infants who were assessed in a modified Strange Situation procedure at age 15 months and then observed in a preschool playgroup for several weeks at age 3½ years. Two a priori sets of items reflecting competence in interpersonal contexts and motivational characteristics that did not assume an interpersonal context were selected from a 72-item Q set and used for a comparison of children who had been classified secure or anxious at 15 months. Scores on the items in each set were summed and used as separate measures. These were designated *social competence* and *ego strength/effectance*. The secure attachment group scored significantly higher than the anxious group on both scales ($\bar{x} = 72.8$ vs. 49.6 [$p < .005$] and $\bar{x} = 79.8$ vs. 68.9 [$p < .05$], respectively). In addition, as indicated in Table 2.5, group differences on every item favored the children who had been classified secure at age 15 months.

These results are consistent with the hypothesis that the attachment relationship supports later social development and has significant longitudinal correlates. Ahrend, Gove, and Sroufe (1979) have also reported competence-related correlates of attachment in children as old as 5 years. Their results also point to the developmental significance of attachment in infancy and directly contradict the predictions from Mischel's (1969) critique of individual differences research

TABLE 2.5

	Item-Total Correlation	Attachment Classification Group Means		One-Tailed t-Test
		Secure	Anxious	
Peer Competence Scale:				
Other children seek his company	.73	6.2	3.8	.001
Socially withdrawn	−.89	3.9	6.2	.002
Suggests activities	.83	6.2	3.5	.005
Hesitates to engage	−.86	3.9	6.2	.007
Peer leader	.71	5.2	3.3	.01
Sympathetic to peers' distress	.43	8.4	4.2	.01
Spectator (vs. participant) in social activities	−.90	4.1	6.1	.02
Attracts attention	.87	5.6	3.4	.02
Hesitant with other children	−.88	3.4	5.4	.03
Withdraws from excitement and commotion	−.49	2.7	4.1	.03
Typically in the role of listener (not full participant in group activities)	−.66	4.2	5.9	.05
Characteristically unoccupied	−.55	3.7	4.7	.14
Ego Strength/Effectance Scale:				
Self-directed	.81	6.4	4.2	.01
Uncurious about the new	−.55	2.4	3.7	.01
Unaware, turned off, "spaced out"	−.78	2.8	4.2	.03
Forcefully goes after what he wants	.67	6.6	5.1	.04
Likes to learn new cognitive skills	.74	5.9	5.0	.05
Confident of his own ability	.58	6.6	5.7	.15
Sets goals which stretch his abilities	.76	6.3	5.5	.19
Becomes involved in whatever he does	.88	7.1	6.5	.23
Does not persevere when nonsocial goals are blocked	−.74	2.7	3.1	.25
Samples activities aimlessly, lacks goals	−.81	3.2	4.8	.25
Suggestible	−.72	4.4	4.8	.36
Indirect in asking for help	−.50	3.2	3.5	.38

and Masters and Wellman's (1974) critique of the attachment construct. They also help us begin to see what is learned in the development and course of an infant-mother relationship. These results do not, however, imply that attachment is necessary for the formation or success of peer relationships in childhood. Indeed a recent study by Furman, Rahe, and Hartup (1979) demonstrates the powerful positive effects that age-mate and cross-age interaction themselves can have on children who experience trouble entering the peer group.

Parental behavior almost certainly makes independent contributions to the development of both attachment and peer relations. Attachment as an outcome of infant-parent interaction, supports the development of peer relations. And peer relations, as influenced by attachment, parent-child interaction, and concurrent peer interactions can play several developmental roles simultaneously. They can be viewed as an outcome of early social experience and studied in their own right. They can be studied as a contribution to later social development. And it is becoming increasingly evident that peer relations can also be viewed as a buffer against the effects of problems in parental behavior and/or infant-parent attachment.

Individual Differences

Recent attachment theory and research have defined an important outcome of parent-infant interaction and have substantially validated effective means for assessing individual differences in attachment relationships. These differences are interesting in themselves and also play important roles as determinants of subsequent child-parent and child-peer interactions. As we have emphasized before, attachment need not always be viewed in an individual differences perspective. The extensive normative data reported by Ainsworth et al. (1978) and by Maccoby and Feldman (1972) attest to this. Nonetheless an individual differences perspective has predominated. When this has resulted from implicit adoption of causal trait models, it has caused problems. When theory and models have been coordinated strategically, the individual differences perspective has been very productive. It will continue to be necessary to employ individual differences research strategies because most theories of the infant-adult bond imply that it arises from some aspects of infant-adult interaction. In order to test these theories in detail and continue the process of construct validation, we shall have to test the hypothesis that differences in parental behavior, infant behavior, and parent-infant interaction result in different outcomes vis-à-vis the infant-adult bond. All normal infants form attachment relationships to one or several caretakers, thus we are left with the natural experiments reflected in variation among individuals. These are the data to which the methodology of individual differences research is well suited. When this methodology is employed to greatest advantage, it can afford important tests of attachment theories and also suggest directions for experimental analyses.

TASKS FOR COMPARATIVE/DEVELOPMENTAL
ANALYSIS

As we have indicated, the systematic examination of alternative models from within theoretical perspectives presents students of the infant–adult bond with a difficult challenge. The review presented herein outlines the importance of meeting this challenge. In concluding we are pointing toward five tasks that deserve high priority in future attachment theory and research. Progress in these should lead to better definition of the attachment construct and facilitate dialogue across the boundaries of theoretical perspective.

1. We are badly in need of better descriptive data concerning the attachment-exploration balance and secure-base phenomenon in humans, nonhuman primates, and in other animals as well. Observations of these phenomena in individuals across reasonable periods of time and in a variety of contexts are almost entirely lacking. Without a substantial descriptive data base both theory and measurement are difficult to advance.

In developing these data it would be useful to integrate it with what is known about the use of conspecifics generally in various species. Indeed it could be very useful for developmentalists to view attachment phenomena as only one example of a variety of multianimal behavioral adaptations.

2. We need to know much more about the roles (plural) of learning in the formation, maintenance, and elaboration of the infant–adult relationship. To say that attachment is learned truly begs the questions "What is attachment?" and "What is learned?" Variables like early physical contact, familiarity, distress, and comforting, species-specific patterns of interaction, cognitive substrates, participation, control, and contingency play important roles for both the parent and the infant. Nonetheless few of these are well defined and when they have been they are not necessarily viewed as one of many factors influencing an exceedingly complex array of things learned. In addition to studying what is learned in the formation of an infant–adult bond, it is important to ask how infant–adult relationships are maintained. It is also important to emphasize that relationships change across time. The learning implicated in acquisition of secure-base behavior does not necessarily explain its maintenance across time or its modification with development and experience. Analysis of the role that first attachments may have on the formation of subsequent attachments is a special interest of ours and promises to help us define some of what is learned during attachment relationships. Our impression is that acquisition of expectations about the efficacy of one's own actions and a variety of other attitude/motivational variables may prove to be more important outcomes than the acquisition of specific skills or behaviors.

3. Ethological attachment theory implies a very strong normative view of infant–adult bonds; that is, infant–adult bonds and the secure-base phenomenon

are predicted to be very similar within and across populations. Learning theories make no such prediction, anticipating instead that relationships will be similar or different insofar as environments (including cultural and behavioral environments) are similar or different. There is clear evidence of species differences in normative patterns of attachment even among primates. These often bear reasonable relationships to the habitats a species typically exploits. This tends to support the notion of a normative pattern of attachment for individual species though the picture would be clearer if we had more descriptive data on variation within populations for a variety of species. At the same time, there is some evidence of ecological variation in patterns of attachment among populations of the same species in different habitats. Only a substantially broader and more detailed comparative description of attachment can enable us to answer the question, "How strong a normative view of infant–adult attachment is appropriate for a given species?" The answer to this question will not necessarily offer a decisive test of ethological versus learning theories, but it would help us place the range of observed individual differences among humans in perspective. It might also allow us to imagine how responsive our normative patterns of attachment would be to changes in social ecology brought on by our own activities. Comparative data can be very relevant to the question, "Is the parental behavior-attachment system a responsive one or does it constitute a behavioral inertia that changes in social ecology would need to accommodate?"

4. Although there are already some preliminary data on relationships between attachment, peer relations, and later personality and social development, we need much more longitudinal research. In undertaking this it will be especially important to recognize changes in attachment, peer relations, and personality with development and to insure age-appropriate assessment throughout the time periods studied. This will involve using different measures to assess the same construct at different ages. In addition it will be important to assess variables like parental behavior, quality of attachment relationships, and relationships to peers repeatedly throughout selected time intervals. In the past the tendency has been to study parental behavior as the cause of attachment or peer relations, attachment as the cause of peer relations, etc. Obviously in the child's experience parental behavior is a continuing influence as is the quality of relationships to the parents and immersion in a peer group. The notion of these as discrete on temporally bounded causes is only a convenient (if sometimes strategically useful) fiction.

5. Finally it is our impression from reviewing the social psychology literature on adult–adult bonds that some issues common to the study of affectional ties at all ages have proven more tractable in studies of infant–adult relationships. It would seem timely to define these common issues and to apply what has been learned about models, measures, continuity, and change from infants to studies of adolescent and adult relationships. This would be the groundwork for studies of infant–adult ties as prototypes of later love relationships. These would include love relationships among adults and perhaps also a parent's love for its offspring.

REFERENCES

Ahrend, R., Gove, F., & Sroufe, L. Continuity of individual adaptation from infancy to kindergarten: A predictive study of ego-resiliency and curiosity in preschoolers. *Child Development,* 1979, *50,* 950–959.

Ainsworth, M. Object relations, dependency, and attachment: A theoretical review of the infant–mother relationship. *Child Development,* 1969, *40,* 969–1025.

Ainsworth, M. Attachment and dependency: A comparison. In J. Gewirtz (Ed.), *Attachment and dependency.* Washington, D.C.: V. H. Winston, 1972.

Ainsworth, M. The development of infant–mother attachment. In B. Caldwell & H. Ricciuti (Eds.), *Review of child development research* (Vol. 3). Chicago: University of Chicago Press, 1973.

Ainsworth, M., Bell, S., & Stayton, D. Individual differences in strange situation behavior of one-year-olds. In H. Schaffer (Ed.), *The origins of human social relations.* London: Academic Press, 1971.

Ainsworth, M., Blehar, M., Waters, E., & Wall, S. *Patterns of attachment.* Hillsdale, N.J.: Lawrence Erlbaum Associates, 1978.

Ainsworth, M., & Witting. B. Attachment and exploratory behavior of one-year-olds in a strange situation. In B. Foss (Ed.), *Determinants of infant behavior* (Vol. 4). New York: Barnes & Noble, 1969.

Baehrends, G. A model of the functional organization of incubation behavior. In G. Baehrends & R. Drent (Eds.), The herring gull and its egg. *Behaviour Supplement,* 1975, *17,* 261–310.

Bertelanffy, L. von. *General systems theory.* New York: Braziller, 1969.

Bischof, N. A systems approach towards the functional connections of fear and attachment. *Child Development,* 1975, *46,* 801–817.

Bowlby, J. *Attachment and loss* (Vol. 1, *Attachment*). New York: Basic Books, 1969.

Bowlby, J. *Attachment and loss* (Vol. 2, *Separation*). New York: Basic Books, 1972.

Cairns, R. *Social development: The origins and plasticity of interchanges.* San Francisco: Freeman, 1979.

Campbell, D., & Fiske, D. Convergent and discriminant validation by the multitrait–multimethod matrix. *Psychological Bulletin,* 1959, *56,* 81–105.

Coates, B., Anderson, E., & Hartup, W. Interrelations in the attachment behavior of human infants. *Developmental Psychology,* 1972 *6,* 218–230. (a)

Coates, B., Anderson, E., & Hartup, W. The stability of attachment behaviors in the human infant. *Developmental Psychology,* 1972, *6,* 231–237.(b)

Cohen, L. The operational definition of human attachment. *Psychological Bulletin,* 1974, *81,* 207–217.

Connell, D. Individual differences in attachment. Unpublished doctoral dissertation, Syracuse University, 1976.

Cronbach, L. Coefficient alpha and the internal structure of tests. *Psychometrika,* 1951, *16,* 297–334.

Cronbach, L., & Meehl, P. Construct validity in psychological tests. *Psychological Bulletin,* 1955, *52,* 281–302.

Furman, W., Rahe, D., & Hartup, W. Rehabilitation of socially withdrawn preschool children through mixed-age and same-age socialization. *Child Development* 1979, *50,* 915–922.

Gewirtz, J. Attachment, dependence, and a distinction in terms of stimulus control. In J. Gewirtz (Ed.), *Attachment and dependency.* Washington, D.C.: V. H. Winston, 1972.(a)

Gewirtz, J. On the selection and use of attachment and dependence indices. In J. Gewirtz (Ed.), *Attachment and dependency.* Washington, D.C.: V. H. Winston, 1972.(b)

Hinde, R. On describing relationships. *Journal of Child Psychology and Psychiatry,* 1976, *17,* 1–19.(a)

Hinde, R. Interactions, relationships, and social structure. *Man,* 1976, 1–17.(b)

Maccoby, E. & Feldman, S. Mother-attachment and stranger-reactions in the third year of life. *Monographs of the Society for Research in Child Development,* 1972, *37* (serial no. 146).

Maccoby, E., & Masters, J. Attachment and dependency. In P. Mussen (Ed.), *Carmichael's manual of child psychology* (Vol. 2). New York: Wiley, 1970.

Magnusson, D. *Test theory*. Reading, Mass.: Addison & Wesley, 1966.

Masters, J. & Wellman, H. Human infant attachment: A procedural critique. *Psychological Bulletin*, 1974, *81*, 218–237.

Miller, G., Galanter, E., & Pribram, K. *Plans and the structure of behavior*. New York: Holt, 1960.

Mischel, W. *Personality and assessment*. New York: McGraw-Hill, 1968.

Mischel, W. Continuity and change in personality. *American Psychologist*, 1969, *24*, 1012–1018.

Mischel, W. Toward a cognitive social learning reconceptualization of personality. *Psychological Review*, 1973, *80*, 252–283.

Nunnally, J. *Psychometric theory* (2nd Ed.). New York: McGraw-Hill, 1978.

Rajecki, D., Lamb, M., & Obmascher, P. Toward a general theory of infantile attachment: A comparative review of aspects of the social bond. *The Behavioral and Brain Sciences*, 1978, *3*, 417–446.

Rosenbaum A. & O'Leary D. Marital violence: characteristics of abusive couples. *Journal of Consulting and Clinical Psychology*, 1981, *49*, 63–71.

Rosenthal, M. Attachment and mother–infant interaction: Some research impasses and a suggested change in orientation. *Journal of Child Psychology and Psychiatry*, 1973, *14*, 201–207.

Rutter, M. *Maternal deprivation: Reassessed*. Baltimore: Penguin Books, 1972.

Sroufe, L., & Waters, E. Attachment as an organizational construct. *Child Development*, 1977, *48*, 1184–1199.

Vaughn, B., Egeland, B., Sroufe, L., & Waters, E. Individual differences in infant–mother attachment at twelve and eighteen months: Stability and change in families under stress. *Child Development*, 1979, *50*, 971–975.

Waters, E. The reliability and stability of individual differences in infant–mother attachment. *Child Development*, 1978, *48*, 489–494.

Waters, E. Traits, behavioral systems, and relationships: Three models of infant–mother attachment. In G. Barlow, K. Immelman, M. Main, & L. Petrinovitch (Eds.), *The development of behavior*. Cambridge: Cambridge University Press, 1980.

Waters, E., Vaughn, B., & Egeland, B. Individual differences in infant–mother attachment: Antecedents in neonatal behavior in an urban economically disadvantaged sample. *Child Development*, 1980, *51*, 208–216.

Waters, E., Wippman, J., & Sroufe, L. Attachment, positive affect and competence in the peer group: Two studies in construct validation. *Child Development*, 1979, *50*, 821–829.

Weinraub, M., Brooks, J., & Lewis, M. The social network: A reconsideration of the concept of attachment. *Human Development*, 1977, *20*, 31–47.

Wiggins, J. *Personality and prediction*. Reading, Mass.: Addison-Wesley, 1973.

Wiggins, J. In defense of traits. Unpublished manuscript. University of British Columbia, 1974.

3

The Father–Child Relationship: A Synthesis of Biological, Evolutionary, and Social Perspectives

Michael E. Lamb
University of Utah
Wendy A. Goldberg
University of Michigan

Our goal in this chapter is to review evidence concerning the origins and nature of parental behavior in human males. In order to achieve this we focus at length upon two related issues: sex differences in parental behavior and the development of parental behavior in species other than our own. We believe that a consideration of biological and evolutionary evidence can sharpen the analysis of parental behavior and parental roles, for as far as species survival is concerned, parental behavior, along with sexual behavior, surely rank as the two most important social activities in any species.

Among vertebrates both types of behavior are characterized by marked sexual dimorphism. Sexual behavior requires the participation of an adult male and an adult female whose roles and responsibilities differ substantially. In most but not all species, breeding is confined to a narrow and fairly well-defined season each year during which one observes males competing over, courting, and impregnating the available females. In most species, the "special relationship" between mating adults does not continue after impregnation.

The nature, extent, and importance of parental behavior are highly variable across the phylogenetic spectrum. The variability is not random, however: It is correlated with the degree to which the young of the species require parental investment in order to survive. Among precocial species, parental responsibilities are usually discharged long before the next breeding season commences, whereas among altricial species far greater proportions of the adults' lives are spent rearing the young. Within the primate order the relationship between infant characteristics and parental behavior is especially clear: As one ascends the order, one finds increasingly prominent stages of infancy and childhood during which special care of the young is necessary if they are to survive. Compared with other primates, the human infant is more helpless and is dependent on adults far longer. As a result, parental behavior is of extreme importance among humans.

Although it is generally recognized that both males and females play crucial and complementary roles in sexual behavior, it has long been presumed that parental behavior is for all intents and purposes the exclusive province of women. The position that has been adopted by social scientists of all persuasions and disciplines was succinctly stated by Margaret Mead: "A father is a biological necessity but a social accident." The mother–infant relationship is typically viewed as one that is of crucial significance to infant development—so important, in fact, that it is buffered against environmentally mediated variation by the evolution of biologically-fixed patterns of behavior. By contrast, the father–child relationship is viewed as a nonessential luxury. This perspective, not coincidentally, assigns scientific and biological credibility to the prejudices and the patterns of childrearing that are currently popular. This may explain why it remained unquestioned until comparatively recently.

The belief that women are innately more nurturant and better suited for childrearing than men are is supported by two kinds of evidence. First, women typically do assume primary responsibility for child care; ergo, this is how men and women are "meant" to behave. Second, maternal behavior within most nonhuman species is presumed to be mediated by the "female" hormones—estrogen, progesterone, and prolactin—and the same hormones are thought to dictate maternal behavior in humans. Both of these arguments are questionable. There is no reason to presume that social practices are innately determined simply because they are widespread, and there is little reason to believe a priori that homologous mechanisms exist in species as different from one another as *rattus* (the most-studied genus) and *homo sapiens*. There is, in any event, no scientific basis for the belief that behavior patterns are inviolable just because biological predispositions exist.

As noted earlier, our plan here is to review and evaluate the evidence and theories concerning maternal and paternal roles in childrearing, synthesizing biological, evolutionary, and social perspectives on this topic. Although we refer repeatedly to evidence concerning other species, our own species is the primary focus throughout. In the first section, we evaluate the claim that hormonal factors and other biological predispositions account for the emergence of species-specific patterns of maternal behavior in parturitional females. The nature and extent of paternal involvement among primates are topics in the next section. Then we turn to evidence concerning biologically-based sex differences in responsiveness to human infants—sex differences that might antedate pregnancy and establish lifelong predispositions in men and women. Thereafter we discuss evidence concerning the relationships that human infants establish with their mothers and fathers.

DETERMINANTS OF MATERNAL BEHAVIOR

Particularly among behavioral biologists, it has long been presumed that behaviors of great importance to species survival will be preorganized in the brains of members of the species. In other words, theorists propose that biological mechanisms ensure the emergence of certain behavior patterns at appropriate points in the animals' lives. In the main, this assumption has fared rather well when subjected to empirical scrutiny. Extensive research on a variety of species has established beyond doubt that hormonal factors play crucial roles in the organization and elicitation of sexual behavior (Bermant & Davidson, 1974). By manipulating hormone levels, particularly in sexually inexperienced animals, it has been possible to affect the sexual propensities of both males and females. Also affected are sex-typed propensities not directly related to courtship and mating.

Hormonal involvement in the establishment and maintenance of parental behavior has been investigated far less extensively and in many fewer species than has sexual behavior. We know a great deal about the hormonal mediation of maternal behavior in laboratory rats however (Lamb, 1975). Research in the laboratories of Rosenblatt, Moltz, and Denenberg has established beyond question that the hormonal events taking place prior to and during parturition prime pregnant females, so that the presence of pups is stimulus enough to elicit well-organized patterns of maternal behavior.

Experiments with rats indicate that the neural basis for maternal behavior (e.g., retrieval of pups, crouching, licking, and nest building) exists in pregnant females, ovariectomized females, hypophysectomized females, virgin females, intact males, and castrated males (Rosenblatt, 1967, 1969, 1970) although a pronounced latency to the onset of such behavior is evident in all but pregnant females. Terkel and Rosenblatt (1968), using chronically-implanted catheters permitting the continuous exchange of blood between parturitional and virgin rats, showed that they could accelerate the emergence of maternal behavior in virgin females. Subsequently, Moltz, Lubin, Leon, and Numan (1970) accelerated the emergence of maternal behavior in virgin females by administering hormones in a sequence mimicking the hormonal changes occurring during gestation. Similar effects were reported by Zarrow, Gandelman, and Denenberg (1971). Thus the importance of hormonal factors in determining the onset of maternal behavior in rats has been well established. It seems that pregnant females are hormonally primed and that this priming accelerates the onset of maternal responsiveness (Adler, 1973). Comparisons of females in early and late pregnancy reveal heightened receptivity to pups among those in late pregnancy (Rosenblatt, 1970). The fact that maternal behavior can be induced in virgin females and in males by prolonged exposure to pups suggests that the neural substrate for maternal behavior exists independent of hormones but that this basis is normally stimulated by hormonal events during pregnancy and parturition. This demonstrates a basic principle concerning the relationship between hormones and behavior; namely that neural sensitivity to the hormones must be present before hormones can function as activators or inhibitors of the neural substrate regulating the behavior (Adler, 1973). Furthermore, although hormones prime the immediate onset of maternal behavior, stimulation from pups is the primary control operating to maintain maternal responsiveness (Adler, 1973; Lamb, 1975). This observation underscores the need to invoke a multilevel perspective in studying the relationship between reproductive hormones and parenting behavior.

Although the relevant research has not been attempted in other species, it is possible that similar mechanisms are responsible for the emergence of parental behavior in primates and rodents. In both orders, hormones are needed to support pregnancy and delay expulsion of the fetus until it is able to survive independently, and these hormonal events could prime the female to behave maternally. Let us briefly review the hormonal changes during gestation, focusing primarily on estrogen, progesterone, and prolactin.

Circulating levels of estrogen and progesterone in pregnant and non-pregnant primates are indistinguishable until 11 days after ovulation (Atkinson, Hotchkiss, Fritz, Surve, Neill, & Knobil, 1975). Major shifts in endocrine activity occur between day 12 and day 40 of gestation. In all mammals, the production of progesterone is vital, since it maintains the uterus in a quiescent state. About 8 days after conception (Hodgen, Dufau, Catt, & Tullner, 1975; Jaffe, 1978), one can first detect secretions of chorionic gonadotropin, a placental protein hormone which maintains the viability of the corpus luteum and thereby stimulates progesterone secretion by the ovaries until the placenta itself can assume this role. Accordingly, levels of chorionic gonadotropin rise quickly, reach a peak 2–3 months after conception, and then rapidly decline to a stable level that is maintained for the remainder of pregnancy (Jaffe, 1978). It follows that regression of the corpus luteum occurs relatively early in primates, and from that point on it no longer plays a role in the maintenance of gestation since the placenta has become a primary site for progesterone secretion (Atkinson et al., 1975). In humans, estriol (an estrogen that is not secreted by the ovaries of nonpregnant women) emerges early and the levels increase as pregnancy advances (Jaffe, 1978). Estriol is a functionally weak estrogen, but it is important for increasing blood flow in the uterus and placenta and thus measures of estriol levels are reliable indications of fetal well-being. Throughout pregnancy, the placenta, fetus, and mother assume complementary roles in the biosynthesis of steroids. Although species differences occur among the primates, these are differences in the magnitude or duration of hormonal levels; the mechanisms remain the same.

Major changes in hormone levels again take place toward the end of pregnancy. Most notably, there is a change in the ratio of estrogen to progesterone. Since estrogen stimulates the release of oxytocin and the prostaglandins which in turn trigger uterine contractions, there is a predictable increase in estrogen in late pregnancy. Levels of urinary estrone rise three-fold during the two weeks prior to parturition, peaking four days before delivery and rapidly declining during the three days preceding birth (Hodgen et al., 1975). Circulating estrogen (estradiol and estrone) levels rise during the last week of gestation (Atkinson et al., 1975; Lanman, 1977) and serum concentration of estradiol in the last three weeks are higher than at any point in the menstrual cycle (Weiss, Butler, Hotchkiss, Dierschke, & Knobil, 1976). Among primates, there are species differences in the pattern of progesterone levels in late pregnancy. In chimpanzees, a second increase occurs about 3/5 of the way through pregnancy, and levels continue to rise until parturition. In macaques, however, progesterone levels are stable throughout most of pregnancy, with a further increase during the final preparturitional week. Prior to parturition, serum progesterone levels decline slightly in marmosets and humans (Lanman, 1977).

Following parturition, estrogen levels fall dramatically to about 4% of preparturitional levels or below the level occurring in the follicular phase of the menstrual cycle (Weiss et al., 1976). These low concentrations of estrogen are maintained at least through 30 days postpartum: They probably reflect low LH and FSH levels caused by the inhibition of gonadotropin secretion by prolactin. Progesterone serum levels also fall after delivery—by about 50%—and the decline continues through the first postpartum month (Weiss et al., 1976). Because progesterone is a lactalbumin inhibitor, the decline in progesterone is necessary if lactation is to occur.

In preparation for lactation, prolactin levels increase fivefold beginning in the last week of pregnancy. Levels of prolactin are at their peak at parturition, gradually declining over the early postpartum period (Weiss et al., 1976). Prolactin stimulates the secretory alveolar cells of the mammary glands, thereby initiating milk synthesis and secretion (Saxena, 1977).

Clearly, these hormonal changes are complex. The greater the number of hormones involved in a particular function and the greater the daily fluctuations in one hormone, the less likely it is that a precise determination of concentration will provide useful information (Doneen, personal communication). Hormonal effects—particularly their effects upon behavior—are poorly understood. Hormonal factors clearly prime pregnant rats and facilitate the emergence of maternal behavior at parturition, it has been proposed that the hormonal changes occurring during gestation have similar effects on primate females. Brandt and Mitchell (1971) note that there are impressive similarities between the delivery-related behavior of various rodent and primate species although there are differences among primate species in the complexity of postpartum behavior. In any event, several investigators have wondered whether there are characteristic patterns of maternal behavior "released" by hormonal triggers around the time of delivery in humans.

The analogy between the effect observed in rats and the effect claimed for primates is problematic. In rats the hormonal changes facilitate the emergence of patterns of behavior that would otherwise not occur for several days. Unlike nulliparous rats, primate adults—and especially human adults—do not ignore newborn infants, and although they may accord priority of access to the neonates' mothers, they are quite capable of behaving "maternally" in the mothers' absence. Nevertheless the search for similarities within the mammalian order has prompted research on initial mother–infant contact.

In an early study, Klaus, Kennell, Plumb, and Zuehlke (1970) reported that when first presented with their newborn infants, human mothers displayed a characteristic pattern of exploratory greeting behavior. Specifically, contacts with the baby initially involved the fingertips but shifted toward the fingers and finally the whole hand and palm. There was also a trend regarding the parts of the infants' bodies with which contact was made: Contact was first made with the infants' extremities—their hands and feet—and only later with their heads and trunks. Speculation that these patterns represented species-specific maternal behavior triggered by the hormonal changes of pregnancy and parturition was fueled by reports that the same patterns of maternal behavior were not evident when infants were delivered prematurely (Klaus et al., 1970). The persuasiveness of the argument is rendered suspect by the finding that comparable patterns of behavior also occur in fathers, who obviously do not experience the hormonal changes of pregnancy and parturition (Rødholm and Larsson, 1979). This suggests that the characteristics of the infants and/or the emotional status of the mothers accounted for the findings obtained with premature infants and their mothers; hormonal status was probably quite unimportant.

By far the most widely cited research on the biological bases of maternal behavior in humans deals with the effects of early contact. On the basis of several studies conducted over the last decade, Klaus and Kennell (1976) claim that the hormonal changes of parturition and pregnancy prime the mother so that she is in a "sensitive period" for the elicitation of maternal behavior in the hours immediately following delivery. If she is permitted several hours of skin-to-skin contact during this period, they argue, one can capitalize upon the sensitive period and thereby ensure that the woman will behave maternally immediately as well as in future interactions with the infant. Mothers permitted early contact with their infants are reported to be more affectionate with and more sensitive to the infants. In other words, early contact is said to facilitate mother-to-infant bonding and thereby promote the healthy development of the infant. In several papers (e.g., Kennell, Jerauld, Wolfe, Chester, Kreger, McAlpine, Steffa, & Klaus, 1974; Klaus, Jerauld, Kreger, McAlpine, Steffa, & Kennell, 1972), Klaus and his colleagues have attempted to document the long-term benefits accruing from the provision of early mother–neonate contact, but there is currently a great deal of controversy concerning the existence of early contact effects, which some researchers have been unable to demonstrate (e.g., Carlsson, Fagerberg, Horneman, Hwang, Larsson, Rødholm, Schaller, Danielsson, & Gundewall, 1978, 1979; Pannabecker & Emde, 1977; Svejda,

Campos & Emde, 1980). We suspect that early contact can indeed be beneficial, but that social-emotional factors—not hormonal ones—are responsible. When considering the relevance of the research on hormone-behavior relationships in rodents, furthermore, it is important to recognize that Klaus and Kennell seek to explain not only the emergence of a set of behaviors but also an emotional process—bonding—which may have implications for later behavior. It is much harder to prove hormonal involvement in such a process, particularly when there is an alternative explanation that appears to us to be more parsimonious and appealing.

In our view both the recent studies critical of Klaus and Kennell's hypothesis as well as the original findings they reported indicate that the bonding of parents to their infants is facilitated by creating a climate at birth that capitalizes upon the exhilaration and emotion of the birth process and recognizes the social importance of childbirth and early parenthood. Currently available evidence does not substantiate the claim that species-specific patterns of behavior are primed by hormonal events and released upon presentation of neonates to new mothers. It seems to us *likely* that although hormonal factors do not prime specific patterns of behavior, they do affect the emotional state and predispositions of parturitional human females. In a sense, then, we agree with a conclusion reached by Ford and Beach (1951) many years ago—namely, that hormones and other biological mechanisms have a more limited effect in humans than in other species. Hormones appear to establish general *predispositions* that depend for their translation into behavior on experiential determinants. As a general rule we propose that hormones facilitate the inhibition or disinhibition of behavior in humans, but they are seldom necessary conditions and are never sufficient in and of themselves. The effects of minor predispositions are reinforced by cultural practices. The vast variability in patterns of human maternal behavior underscores the degree to which individual experiences are major determinants of parental behavior.

Parental behavior in humans must surely rank as one of the clearest examples of overdetermined behavior. In addition to hormonal influences, each young woman is subjected to many years of socializing pressures preparing her for the maternal role. In many "primitive" societies, the preparations involve considerable experience caring for young infants. The supportiveness and respectfulness of the atmosphere created by delivery room personnel can dampen or accentuate the affective tone of childbirth, thus determining whether or not the new parents can express their emotions to one another and to the object of their emotions—the newborn infant. In the midst of such a complex and comprehensive set of influences, it seems unlikely that hormonal influences make unique and independent contributions to the emergence of parental behavior in humans.

In other words, if hormonal influences do render women better prepared and suited for parental behavior than men, this advantage is secured largely by way of an extensive overlay of socialization. If boys and girls were given equal exposure to infants and were equivalently prepared for parenthood, we doubt that any systematic sex differences in parental behavior would be found. This illustrates a more general rule concerning the nature of biological predispositions among humans: Their potency is established and multiplied by societal practices that capitalize upon and exaggerate minor behavioral tendencies and so render universal sex-differentiated behavior patterns that would scarcely be noticeable in the absence of supplementary socialization. This argument, of course, applies to the emergence of characteristic patterns of paternal behavior just as it applies to the emergence of maternal behavior.

PATERNAL INVOLVEMENT IN PRIMATES

In the foregoing pages, we have focused exclusively on the determinants and nature of maternal behavior. Let us now review briefly what little is known about "paternalistic" behavior in primates. More detailed reviews have been published by Mitchell (1969), Mitchell and Brandt (1972), and Redican (1976).

The behavior of adult males toward infants is even more variable among nonhuman primates than it is among humans. It ranges from tolerantly ignoring on the one extreme to primary responsibility for infant care on the other. In their review, Mitchell and Brandt (1972) distinguish among 10 levels of interaction: no interactions at all, toleration, touching, carrying, approaching, retrieving, grooming/playing, protecting, caring for, and adopting. About the only response that is characteristic of males in all primate species is the tendency to defend infants against aggression, especially when the aggressive individual is an intruder.

There is no apparent consistency to the variability in paternal behavior among different primate species: No single factor appears necessary and sufficient to ensure high paternal involvement. There is neither an increase nor a decrease as one "ascends" the primate order, even though one might expect that with the increasing dependency of infants males would assume more responsibility. Degree of involvement also appears unrelated to characteristics of the species' ecological niche because there are instances of both high and low involvement among both tree- and ground-dwelling species. Although the highest degree of male involvement occurs in a species (marmosets) in which multiple births are the norm, this factor is clearly not crucial because lemurs (who also have multiple births) are characterized by extremely low degrees of male involvement. One species characteristic that appears to be "necessary but not sufficient" to ensure higher male involvement is the prevalence of monogamous male–female relationships. Males also tend to be more positively disposed toward infants in polygamous (but not in polyandrous) species. It has been suggested that androgen withdrawal, or a shift in the androgen/estrogen ratio favoring estrogens may be partly responsible for seasonal changes in paternalistic behavior (Alexander, 1970). Unfortunately, however, there has been little research on the relationship between hormonal factors and parental behavior in primate males.

The variability existing among primates prevents us from identifying an evolutionary or phylogenetic trend in the degree of male involvement with infants and juveniles. Among the higher primates there is consistency to the extent that females universally assume primary responsibility for child care whereas males are at best marginally involved. Even in these species, however, males appear capable of more solicitous relations when the circumstances demand it (Redican, 1976).

Paternal involvement in child care is most extensive among several species of New World monkeys, notably marmosets (callithrix, pygmy, tamarin), titi, and night monkeys. Adult males in these species share or dominate parenting roles, especially with first offspring (Redican, 1976). Marmosets are by no means typical of primate species, but their "family roles" raise further doubts about simplistic notions concerning hormone-behavior relationships. Three things are especially noteworthy: (1) marmosets are essentially monogamous; (2) they typically produce twins (and sometimes triplets), which is rare among most primate species; and (3) primary responsibility for child care is assumed by the infants' fathers. Mothers take over offspring for nursing only. Otherwise the infants are carried by their fathers, are introduced to solid food by their fathers, and spend most of their time with them. Among callithrix marmosets (Brandt & Mitchell, 1971) fathers assist in parturition by receiving and washing the infants and assuming care of neonates. Interestingly, paternal involvement is greatest with firstborn twins; with later births males are often less involved as older siblings are able to assume a major role (Redican, 1976). In most respects marmoset females behave much like males behave in other species: They rebuff infant initiatives and cuff infants attempting to share their food (Redican, 1979). Clearly, whatever predispositions are established by the hormonal variations of pregnancy and parturition are overridden by social factors in this species. There is every reason to believe that human predispositions could be overridden in comparable fashion.

RESPONSIVENESS TO INFANTS IN HUMAN MEN AND WOMEN

As we are all aware, the arrangement that has worked for marmosets differs markedly from the caretaking practices characteristic of human parents. There are few societies in the world in which fathers assume more than a token responsibility for child care. In the main, caretaking is viewed as the exclusive province of women. In "primitive" societies, adult women contribute to the family economy by child rearing and by undertaking those agricultural and household responsibilities that can be performed in combination with infant and child care. Men generally assume responsibility for those activities that cannot be combined with parenting, but even when they are physically present and unoccupied, men in both primitive and modern societies assume little responsibility for child care. In this section we are concerned with speculations regarding sex differences in responsiveness to infants across the life span. We ask whether sex differences in responsiveness to infants exist and if so whether they are innate, attributable to current circulating levels of crucial hormones (testosterone and estrogen), or to socializing pressures and expectations. A more comprehensive discussion than ours has been provided by Berman (1980): We shall only cite and discuss especially pertinent or revealing findings.

Sex differences in responsiveness to infants have been explored in three ways. Some researchers have gathered behavioral data, others have employed psychophysiological techniques, whereas others have employed self-report procedures. In general the findings point toward a consistent and coherent conclusion. Similar conclusions are reached regardless of whether the subjects are parents (responding to their own or to unfamiliar infants), grandparents, or children in middle childhood or early adolescence.

Let us first consider the evidence gathered by Ross Parke and his colleagues. Over the last decade Parke has conducted several studies in which mothers and fathers are observed interacting with their own newborn infants. In the first such study (Parke & O'Leary, 1976), the observations took place in maternity wards and involved as subjects men and women who had only recently become parents. The study showed that both mothers and fathers behaved with equivalent activity and enthusiasm in interaction with their young infants. In a later study observations were made at home, and a new observational technique made it possible to assess, not only the frequency of various parental behaviors, but their contingency in relation to the infants' behavior as well (Parke & Sawin, 1977). When feeding their infants, Parke and Sawin reported, mothers and fathers were equivalently likely to respond to the infants' signals and behaviors although they tended to respond with somewhat different behaviors. Evidently there were no sex differences in parents' responsiveness to infant signals even though the mothers were primary caretakers and assumed responsibility for the infants' care even when fathers were available.

We have focused our attention upon the parents' physiological responses to infants' smiles and cries. Following Lamb (1978b), we have argued that the function of infants' cries was to arouse caretakers and encourage them to engage in behaviors likely to eliminate the infants' distress (see also Murray, 1979). Because cries should elicit from adults behavior aimed at termination of the signal, we reasoned that the signals themselves should be perceived as aversive and arousing. The function of smiles, meanwhile, is to encourage adults to remain in interaction with and in proximity to the infants; as a result, smiles should be perceived as pleasant and relaxing stimuli. This is precisely what Frodi, Lamb, Leavitt, and Donovan (1978) found in their first study. In response to the sight and sound of a crying infant, increases in psychophysiological indices of arousal were recorded, and the subjects reported that they found the cry aversive and irritating. By contrast, when the participants viewed a smiling and cooing infant, there occurred minor and sometimes insignificant declines in levels of psychophysiological arousal and positive moods were reported (Frodi,

Lamb, Leavitt, & Donovan, 1978). For the present purposes, it is especially important to note that in two large studies (Frodi, Lamb, Leavitt, & Donovan, 1978; Frodi, Lamb, Leavitt, Donovan, Neff, & Sherry, 1978), Frodi and her colleagues found no sex differences on the measures of physiological responsiveness: Mothers and fathers evinced similar physiological responses although the mothers reported more extreme emotions. Using the same paradigm, Frodi and Lamb (1978) reported no sex differences in responsiveness to infants among 8- and 14-year-old children.

The findings of Frodi and her colleagues contradict the notion that biological factors account for large and significant differences in the responsiveness of men and women to infants and infant signals. Socialization pressures appeared to be far more important. Direct tests of this hypothesis have been attempted by Feldman and her colleagues (Abraham, Feldman, & Nash, 1978; Feldman & Nash, 1979; Feldman, Nash, & Cutrona, 1977) as well as by Frodi and Lamb (1978). Feldman and Nash have repeatedly found that sex differences wax and wane depending on whether the subjects are in a stage of the life span wherein there is an intensification of pressures to evince traditionally sex-stereotyped behavior. Thus new mothers are more responsive than new fathers, and teenage girls are more responsive than teenage boys, whereas no sex differences are found among college students, young adults, and childless married or cohabiting adults. Feldman and Nash point out that teenagers and parents are under pressure to conform to traditional sex roles, and suggest that these pressures, rather than the hormonal events occuring at these times, account for the emergence of sex differences in responsiveness. The claim that social pressures, not biological predispositions, account for sex differences in responsiveness to infants was further reinforced by Frodi and Lamb (1978). They demonstrated that the same children who showed no sex differences on psychophysiological measures of responsiveness evinced "sex-appropriate" behavior when observed in an experimental situation like Feldman's. On more covert or more physiological measures, in other words, sex differences were absent whereas on overt behavioral indices, sex differences were evident. Finally, Berman, Abplanalp, Cooper, Mansfield, and Shields (1975) found that men and women reported more attraction to babies when in same sex groups than in mixed sex groups and that public disclosure of ratings led women to express greater attraction, and men less attraction, toward infants.

The absence of innate differences in responsiveness to infants suggests that mothers and fathers are equivalently capable of assuming formatively significant roles in their infants' social development. Of course we know that in most societies, men leave women to assume primary child care responsibilities. It appears, furthermore, that this pattern is unlikely to change much in the foreseeable future. Despite the publicity accorded to role-reversing families, their numbers are few and their circumstances unique. Closer inspection, furthermore, reveals that they usually involve reversed roles in the rearing of school-aged children: Infant care, even in these families, typically remains the province of mothers. The widespread entry by women into the labor force appears to have had a marginal impact on the relative responsibilities of men and women for child care and parenting (cf. Hoffman, 1977). The "modified traditional pattern"—to use Komarovsky's term—probably represents as great a deviation from traditional practices as we can expect to occur in the foreseeable future. Most of the male college students interviewed by Komarovsky (1976, 1979) endorsed such a pattern, which involves women pausing in the career trajectory in order to bear and rear children before returning to work. For this reason, it remains relevant to consider evidence concerning the development of mother- and father-infant relations in traditional families.

FATHER–INFANT INTERACTIONS IN HUMANS

Let us shift our attention, therefore, from the macrosocietal to the individual level of analysis, asking how infant development is affected by the assumption of traditional parental roles. From the infant's perspective, the social world is dominated by its mother though she is certainly not the exclusive component. Interactions with father are certain to be far less extensive than those with mother. Parke and Sawin's (1977) data are pertinent: Mothers and fathers were equivalently competent and responsive as caretakers, but the fathers tended to leave child care to their wives even when they were present. There is disagreement concerning the extent of father–infant interactions, but none of the relevant studies (e.g., Kotelchuck, 1972; Pedersen & Robson, 1969) suggest that father–infant interaction exceeds an average of 10 hours per week. The amount of time that fathers and babies are both awake and in the same house (but not in interaction) must be far more extensive than this of course.

Perhaps the first question to attract attention in this area was whether or not infants and their fathers spent enough time together so that infant–father attachments could develop. The first attempt to answer this question empirically was made by Schaffer and Emerson (1964) who asked mothers to estimate the probability that infants would be distressed when separated briefly from a number of familiar people, including mothers and fathers. Schaffer and Emerson found that many infants were attached to (i.e., protested separation from) both parents by 9 months of age and that the majority were so attached by 18 months of age. Pedersen and Robson (1969), relying on maternal reports of the probability of positive greeting responses, confirmed Schaffer and Emerson's conclusion.

The first observational studies of mother–infant and father–infant interaction took place in the 1970s. Most of these studies involved observations of families in structured laboratory settings and all confirmed that, at least by 12 months of age (which appeared to be the youngest age about which meaningful data could be obtained in the laboratory), most infants have formed attachments to both their mothers and their fathers. Kotelchuck and his colleagues (Kotelchuck, 1972,

1976; Ross, Kagan, Zelazo, & Kotelchuck, 1975; Spelke, Zelazo, Kagan, & Kotelchuck, 1973) reached this conclusion on the basis of several studies of infant reactions to brief separations from their parents in the laboratory. Similar conclusions were reached by Cohen and Campos (1974), Feldman and Ingham (1975) and Willemsen, Flaherty, Heaton, and Ritchey (1974). In each case, young infants clearly discriminated between their parents and unfamiliar adults, and they consistently showed a preference for the two parents over the comparison figure.

Compared with the large number of laboratory studies, there have been few studies of parent–infant interactions in the naturalistic home setting. Among these was a longitudinal study by Lamb (1976b, 1977a, 1977c) focused on the display of attachment or proximity-promoting behaviors to mothers and fathers. The conclusion was similar to that reached by those conducting research in laboratories: Attachment behaviors were rarely directed to unfamiliar persons, even when they were available and were interacting amicably with the infants. The fact that these behaviors were focused on the parents suggested that it was these persons to whom the infants were attached (Ainsworth, 1964). In the stress-free home environment, no preferences for either parent over the other were evident from 7 months of age—the age at which infants should have been forming their first social attachments (Bowlby, 1969).

In addition to repeated home observations the subjects in this study were also observed under more stressful circumstances in the laboratory. Both 12- and 18-month-olds, Lamb (1976a, 1976d) found, turned to their mothers by preference when they were distressed and when they had a choice between the two parents. When both parents were not present, infants organized their attachment behavior similarly around whichever parent accompanied them. Lamb concluded from these data that the infants were clearly attached to both parents although their primary attachment relationships were with their primary caretakers. Most of the attempts to investigate preferences for one parent over the other, Lamb (1978a) argued, point toward a similar conclusion although Parke (1979) perceives less clarity and greater inconsistency. Parke and Lamb, as well as the others who have undertaken observational studies of father–infant interaction (Belsky, 1979; Clarke-Stewart, 1978), are in agreement that infants typically develop attachment relationships to both parents.

Having accepted that conclusion, several psychologists then sought to determine whether the mother–infant and father–infant relationships involved different types of interactions and experiences. The answer is clearly affirmative. Because they assume the role as primary caretaker, mothers' interactions with their infants are characterized by involvement in caretaking routines far more than father–infant relations are (Belsky, 1979; Lamb, 1976b, 1977c). With mothers associated in the infant's mind with caretaking, meanwhile, fathers may become known for the stimulating and playful nature of their interactions, although the data here are less clear than they are regarding caretaking involvement. Lamb (1976b, 1977c) found that mothers and fathers initiated about as much play with their infants but that paternal play tended to be boisterous and physically stimulating. Maternal play was more likely to involve toys or conventional (ritualized) routines. In an interview study conducted in Australia, Russell (1978) replicated these findings concerning the nature of maternal and paternal interaction styles. Probably because the categories of play were inappropriate for older infants, Belsky (1979) found no significant differences between maternal and paternal play styles in 15-month-old infants. Interestingly, the infants in Lamb's study also responded more positively to play with their fathers, and Clarke-Stewart (1978) reported that 15-30-month-olds were significantly more responsive to play initiated by fathers than by mothers. In a structured play situation, her subjects were more cooperative, interested, and involved in play with their fathers. It seems, therefore, that fathers become identified as special playmates fairly early in infancy, presumably because the way they play as well as their relatively novelty makes them more exciting social partners than mothers are. Evidently the fact that parents assume sex-differentiated roles in relation to their infants has implications for the type of relationships infants develop with them and the expectations they have of them. This implies that mothers and fathers probably contribute in different ways to their infants' development.

Sex Differences in Father-Child Relations

Long before Freud (1905/1962) popularized the notion, it was presumed that fathers had a special role to play in sex-role socialization—especially of their sons. It was not until recently, however, that we realized how early this special role became apparent.

As indicated before, Lamb (1977a, 1977c) found no preference for either parent over the other during the first year of life. During the second year, however, attachment behavior measures showed significant preferences on these measures for fathers over mothers. These preferences reflected a major sex difference. During the first year boys and girls behaved very similarly, whereas from the beginning of the second year of life the boys began to show preferences for their fathers. A comparable preference on the part of girls for their mothers was much weaker.

Lamb (1977b) then reanalyzed the data, focusing on the emergence of preferences in individual infants. He reported that by the end of the second year, eight of the nine male infants remaining in his sample were showing a consistent preference for their fathers, whereas among the girls the plurality preferred their mothers, some preferred their fathers, and some preferred neither parent consistently.

The focalization of boys upon their fathers appeared to be caused by a change in the fathers' behavior—a change that involved a dramatic increase in the amount of attention they paid to their sons. As pointed out in an earlier review

(Lamb, 1978a), these findings are consistent with other reports that fathers are more eager to interact with sons than with daughters and that boys are increasingly likely to develop preferential relationships with their fathers as they grow older. Stereotyping pressures on girls are usually far less intensive and begin far later than the equivalent pressures on boys (Lamb, 1976c).

There are two reasons to believe that the father–infant relationship may indeed be especially important in the second year of life. First, there is evidence that father absence has its greatest and most predictable effects when the father leaves earlier in the child's life (Biller, 1974, 1976). Second, John Money has argued that gender identity is most readily and securely established during the first 3 years of life (Money & Ehrhardt, 1972). Because the change in paternal behavior is the most obvious event during this period, it is tempting to speculate that it may be involved in the establishment of gender identity.

THE DETERMINANTS OF PATERNAL BEHAVIOR

There is clear evidence, in sum, not only that fathers behave in a distinctive fashion, but that the paternal role may be formatively significant. The assumption by fathers of a traditional paternal role in the family serves to facilitate the socialization of children into gender roles and gender identities. The fathers themselves, of course, were affected by similar processes of socialization, and these surely influence the way in which they behave as male adults and as fathers. While noting the extensiveness of sex-differentiating socialization, however, it is important to recall that experiential determinants of behavior often coexist with or complement biological determinants. Again we wonder how biological predispositions affect the manner in which parental responsibilities are typically divided between men and women.

Two types of biologically-determined predispositions are possible. First, women may be predisposed to respond more nurturantly and "parentally" than men do. There is no direct evidence available to support this argument, which is based on data obtained in research on several—particularly rodent—species. It is necessary to build a case here upon analogy and the case is weakened by the facts that parental behavior is more complex in humans than in rats and that parental behavior is often displayed by nulliparous women and men (babysitters, day care attendants, etc.). Parental behavior does not occur spontaneously in rats. There is also no evidence that variations in the levels of the female hormones—estrogens, progesterone, and prolactin—have specific effects on parental behavior in humans. On the other hand, the evidence regarding hormonal effects in other species is so strong that hormone-behavior relationships, albeit complex ones, probably exist in humans as well.

An alternative type of biological predisposition might involve a relationship between the "male" hormones—the androgens and testosterone— and behavioral dispositions (e.g., aggressiveness) that are inimical to optimal infant care. There is in fact general agreement that testosterone levels are related in a nonmonotonic fashion to physical aggressiveness and activity level (Maccoby & Jacklin, 1974) and this lends credence to the argument. On the other hand, there is evidence that the young of most species are rendered immune from attacks by adults by virtue of certain infantile characteristics (Jolly, 1972; Lorenz, 1935/ 1970). Furthermore the behavior of marmosets is once again germane: Clearly, males can behave nurturantly whatever their predispositions and internal hormonal state.

There is, therefore, no direct evidence regarding biologically–determined sex differences in the potential for displaying parental behavior among humans, and the circumstantial evidence available indicates that whatever predispositions exist are slight. These caveats notwithstanding, we lean toward the conclusion that some biologically based predispositions probably exist. The universal differentiation of maternal and paternal roles has probably come about because social practices have built upon these biological predispositions, thus exaggerating the differences and producing societies in which gender-differentiated behavior is the norm. These predispositions may make it minimally easier for females to learn how to behave parentally, but they set neither ceilings nor floors to the potential of either males or females. Given the appropriate training and experience, men and women can be equivalently good as parents—behaviorally and emotionally.

In these days of irresponsible comparative generalization we need to underscore the fact that sex-differentiated predispositions are by no means inviolable. As a species, we have already deviated from countless tendencies or predispositions. "Violations of natural tendencies" pass without comment unless social and political sensibilities are questioned: Then appeals to "natural laws" provide a comfortable rationale for resistance. In the absence today of the circumstances that made gender-role differentiation reasonable in past ecologies (for example, the invention of the nursing bottle makes breastfeeding discretionary rather than mandatory), there is enormous potential for deviation from innate predispositions, and we believe that there is every justification for such "deviations." Human boys and girls could undoubtedly be socialized such that maternal and paternal roles were reversed. The fact that this has not happened (and probably will not happen) may be attributed to societal inertia, not to our evolutionary heritage.

REFERENCES

Abraham, B., Feldman, S. S., & Nash, S. C. Sex role self-concept and sex role attitudes: Enduring personality characteristics or adaptations to changing life situations? *Developmental Psychology*, 1978, *14*, 393–400.

Adler, N. The biopsychology of hormones and behavior. In D. A. Dewbury & D. A. Rethlingshafer (Eds.), *Comparative psychology: A modern survey.* New York: McGraw-Hill, 1973.

Ainsworth, M. Patterns of attachment behavior shown by the infant in interaction with his mother. *Merrill–Palmer Quarterly*, 1964, *10*, 51-58.

Alexander, B. Parental care of adult male Japanese monkeys. *Behaviour*, 1970, *36*, 270-285.

Atkinson, L., Hotchkiss, J., Fritz, G., Surve, A., Neill, J., & Knobil, E. Circulating levels of steroids and chorionic gonadotropin during pregnancy in the rhesus monkey with special attention to the rescue of the corpus luteum in early pregnancy. *Biology of Reproduction*, 1975, *12*. 335.

Belsky, J. Mother–father–infant interaction: A naturalistic observational study. *Developmental Psychology*, 1979, *15*, 601-607.

Berman, P. Are women predisposed to parenting? Developmental and situational determinants of sex differences in responsiveness to the young. *Psychological Bulletin*, 1980, *88*, 668-695.

Berman, P., Abplanalp, P., Cooper, Mansfield, P., & Shields, S. Sex differences in attraction to infants: When do they occur? *Sex Roles*, 1975, *1*, 311-315.

Bermant, G., & Davidson, J. *Biological bases of sexual behavior*. New York: Harper & Row, 1974.

Bielert, T., Czaja, J., Eisele, S., Scheffler, G., Robinson, J., & Goy, R. Mating in the rhesus monkey after conception and its relationship to estradiol and progesterone levels throughout pregnancy. *Journal of Reproduction and Fertility*, 1976, *46*, 179.

Biller, H. Paternal deprivation, cognitive functioning, and the feminized classroom. In A. Davids (Ed.), *Child personality and psychopathology: Current Topics* (Vol. 1). New York: Wiley, 1974.

Biller, H. The father and personality development: Paternal deprivation and sex role development. In M. E. Lamb (Ed.), *The role of the father in child development*. New York: Wiley, 1976.

Bowlby, J. *Attachment*. New York: Basic Books, 1969.

Brandt, E., & Mitchell, G. Parturition in primates: Behavior related to birth. In L. Rosenblum (Ed.), *Primate Behavior*. New York: Academic Press, 1971.

Carlsson, S., Fagerberg, H., Horneman, G., Hwang, C-P., Larsson, K., Rødholm, M., Schaller, J., Danielsson, B., & Gundewall, C. Effects of amount of contact between mother and child on the mother's nursing behavior. *Developmental Psychobiology*, 1978, *11*, 143-150.

Carlsson, S., Fagerberg, H., Horneman, G., Hwang, C-P., Larsson, K., Rødholm, M., Schaller, J., Danielsson, B., & Gundewall, C. Effects of various amounts of contact between mother and child on the mother's nursing behavior: A follow-up study. *Infant Behavior and Development*, 1979, *2*, 209-214.

Clarke-Stewart, K. A. And daddy makes three: The father's impact on mother and young child. *Child Development*, 1978, *49*, 466-478.

Cohen, L. J., & Campos, J. J. Father, mother, and stranger as elicitors of attachment behaviors in infancy. *Developmental Psychology*, 1974, *10*, 146-154.

Feldman, S. S., & Ingham, M. Attachment behavior: A validation study in two age groups. *Child Development*, 1975, *46*, 319-330.

Feldman, S. S., & Nash. S. C. Interest in babies during young adulthood. *Child Development*, 1978, *49*, 617-622.

Feldman, S. S., & Nash, S. C. Understanding responsiveness to babies among mature adults. Paper presented to the Society for Research in Child Development, San Francisco, March 1979.

Feldman, S. S., Nash, S. C., & Cutrona, C. The influence of age and sex on responsiveness to babies. *Developmental Psychology*, 1977, *13*, 656-657.

Ford, C., & Beach, F. A. *Patterns of sexual behavior*. New York: Harper, 1951.

Freud, S. *Three essays on the theory of sexuality* (1905). New York: Avon, 1962.

Frodi, A. M., & Lamb, M. E. Sex differences in responsiveness to infants: A developmental study of psychophysiological and behavioral responses. *Child Development*, 1978, *49*, 1182-1188.

Frodi, A. M., Lamb, M. E., Leavitt, L. A., & Donovan, W. L. Fathers' and mothers' responses to infant smiles and cries. *Infant Behavior and Development*, 1978, *1*, 187-198.

Frodi, A. M., Lamb, M. E., Leavitt, L. A., Donovan, W. L., Neff, C., & Sherry, D. Fathers' and mothers' responses to the faces and cries of normal and premature infants. *Developmental Psychology*, 1978, *14*, 490-498.

Hodgen, G., Dufau, L., Catt, K., & Tullner, W. Estrogen, progesterone, and chorionic gonadotropin in pregnant rhesus monkeys. *Endocrinology,* 1975, *91,* 896.

Hoffman, L. W. Changes in family roles, socialization, and sex differences. *American Psychologist,* 1977, *32,* 644–657.

Jolly, A. *The evolution of primate behavior.* New York: Macmillan, 1972.

Kennell, J., Jerauld, R., Wolfe, H., Chester, D., Kreger, N., McAlpine, W., Steffa, M., & Klaus, M. Maternal behavior one year after early and extended post-partum contact. *Developmental Medicine and Child Neurology,* 1974, *16,* 172–179.

Klaus, M., Jerauld, R., Kreger, N., McAlpine, W., Steffa, M., & Kennell, J. Maternal attachment: importance of the first post-partum days. *New England Journal of Medicine,* 1972, *286,* 460–463.

Klaus, M., & Kennell, J. *Maternal–infant bonding.* St. Louis, Mo: C. V. Mosby, 1976.

Klaus, M., Kennell, J., Plumb, N., & Zuehlke, S. Human maternal behavior at first contact with her young. *Pediatrics,* 1970, *46,* 187–192.

Komarovsky, M. *Dilemmas of masculinity: A study of college youth.* New York: Norton, 1976.

Komarovsky, M. Dilemmas of masculinity in a changing world. In J. E. Gullahorn (Ed.), *Psychology and women: In transition.* New York: Winston, 1979.

Kotelchuck, M. The nature of the child's tie to his father. Unpublished doctoral dissertation, Harvard University, 1972.

Kotelchuck, M. The infant's relationship to the father: Experimental evidence. In M. E. Lamb (Ed.), *The role of the father in child development.* New York: Wiley, 1976.

Lamb, M. E. Physiological mechanisms in the control of maternal behavior in rats: A review. *Psychological Bulletin,* 1975, *82,* 104–119.

Lamb, M. E. Effects of stress and cohort on mother- and father-infant interaction. *Developmental Psychology,* 1976, *12,* 435–443. (a)

Lamb, M. E. Interactions between eight-month-old children and their fathers and mothers. In M. E. Lamb (Ed.), *The role of the father in child development.* New York: Wiley, 1976. (b)

Lamb, M. E. The role of the father: An overview. In M. E. Lamb (Ed.), *The role of the father in child development.* New York: Wiley, 1976. (c)

Lamb, M. E. Twelve-month-olds and their parents: Interaction in a laboratory playroom. *Developmental Psychology,* 1976, *12,* 237–244. (d)

Lamb, M. E. The development of mother–infant and father–infant attachments in the second year of life. *Developmental Psychology,* 1977, *13,* 637–648. (a)

Lamb, M. E. The development of parental preferences in the first two years of life. *Sex Roles,* 1977, *3,* 495–497. (b)

Lamb, M. E. Father–infant and mother–infant interaction in the first year of life. *Child Development,* 1977, *48,* 167–181. (c)

Lamb, M. E. The father's role in the infant's social world. In J. H. Stevens & M. Mathews (Eds.), *Mother/child, father/child relationships.* Washington, D.C.: National Association for the Education of Young Children, 1978. (a)

Lamb, M. E. The influence of the child on marital quality and family interaction during the prenatal, paranatal, and infancy periods. In R. M. Lerner & G. B. Spanier (Eds.), *Child influences on marital and family interaction: A lifespan perspective.* New York: Academic, 1978. (b)

Lanman, J. Parturition in nonhuman primates. *Biology of Reproduction,* 1977, *16,* 28–38.

Lorenz, K. The conspecific as the eliciting factor for social behavior patterns (1935). In K. Lorenz (Ed.), *Studies in animal and human behavior* (Vol. 1). Cambridge, Mass.: Harvard University Press, 1970.

Maccoby, E. E., & Jacklin, C. N. *The psychology of sex differences.* Stanford, Cal.: Stanford University Press, 1974.

Mitchell, G. Paternalistic behavior in primates. *Psychological Bulletin,* 1969, *71,* 399–417.

Mitchell, G., & Brandt, E. Paternal behavior in primates. In F. Poirier (Ed.), *Primate socialization.* New York: Random House, 1972.

Moltz, H., Lubin, M., Leon, M., & Numan, M. Hormonal induction of maternal behavior in the ovariectomized nulliparous rat. *Physiology and Behavior,* 1970, *5,* 1373–1377.

Money, J., & Ehrhardt, A. *Man and Women, Boy and Girl.* Baltimore, Md.: Johns Hopkins University Press, 1972.

Murray, A. Infant crying as an elicitor of parental behavior: An examination of two models. *Psychological Bulletin,* 1979, *86,* 191–215.

Pannabecker, B. J., & Emde, R. The effect of extended contact on father–newborn interaction. Paper presented at the Tenth Annual Communicating Nursing Research Conference, Western Society for Research in Nursing, Denver, Colorado, May 1977.

Parke, R. Perspectives on father–infant interaction. In J. D. Osofsky (Ed.), *Handbook of infant development.* New York: Wiley, 1979.

Parke, R. D., & O'Leary, S. Father–mother–infant interaction in the newborn period: Some findings, some observations, and some unresolved issues. In K. Riegel & J. Meacham (Eds.), *The developing individual in a changing world* (Vol. 2). *Social and environmental issues.* The Hague: Mouton, 1976.

Parke, R. D., & Sawin, D. The family in early infancy: Social interactional and attitudinal analyses. Paper presented to the Society for Research in Child Development, New Orleans, March 1977.

Pedersen, F., & Robson, K. Father participation in infancy. *American Journal of Orthopsychiatry,* 1969, *39,* 466–472.

Redican, W. Adult-male–infant interactions in nonhuman primates. In M. E. Lamb (Ed.), *The role of the father in child development.* New York: Wiley, 1976.

Redican, W. Personal communication, March 1979.

Rødholm, M., & Larsson, K. Father–infant interaction at the first contact after delivery. *Early Human Development,* 1979, *3,* 21–27.

Rosenblatt, J. S. Nonhormonal basis of maternal behavior in the rat. *Science,* 1967, *156,* 1512–1514.

Rosenblatt, J. S. The development of maternal responsiveness in the rat. *American Journal of Orthopsychiatry,* 1969, *39,* 36–56.

Rosenblatt, J. S. Views on the onset and maintenance of maternal behavior in the rat. In L. R. Aronson, E. Tobach, D. S. Lehrman & J. S. Rosenblatt (Eds.), *Development and evolution of behavior: Essays in memory of T. C. Schneirla.* San Francisco: Freeman, 1970.

Ross, G., Kagan, J., Zelazo, P., & Kotelchuck, M. Separation protest in infants in home and laboratory. *Developmental Psychology,* 1975, *11,* 256–257.

Russell, G. The father role and its relation to masculinity, femininity, and androgyny. *Child Development,* 1978, *49,* 1174–1181.

Saxena, J. Human prolactin. In F. Fuchs & A. Klopper (Eds.), *Endocrinology of pregnancy.* New York: Harper & Row, 1977.

Schaffer, H., & Emerson, P. The development of social attachments in infancy. *Monographs of the Society for Research in Child Development,* 1964, *29,* (whole number 94).

Spelke, E., Zelazo, P., Kagan, J., & Kotelchuck, M. Father interaction and separation protest. *Developmental Psychology,* 1973, *9,* 83–90.

Svejda, M. J., Campos, J. J., & Emde, R. N. Mother–infant ''bonding'': Failure to generalize. *Child Development,* 1980, *51,* 775–779.

Terkel, J., & Rosenblatt, J. S. Maternal behavior induced by maternal blood plasma injected into virgin rats. *Journal of Comparative and Physiological Psychology,* 1968, *65,* 479–482.

Weiss, G., Butler, W., Hotchkiss, J., Dierschke, D., & Knobil, E. Periparturitional serum concentrations of prolactin, the gonadotropins, and the gonadal hormones in the rhesus monkey. *Proceedings of the Society for Experimental Biological Medicine,* 1976, *151,* 113–116.

Willemsen, E., Flaherty, D., Heaton, C., & Ritchey, G. Attachment behavior of one-year-olds as a function of mother vs. father, sex of child, session, and toys. *Genetic Psychology Monographs,* 1974, *90,* 305–324.

Zarrow, M., Gandelman, R., & Denenberg, V. H. Prolactin: Is it an essential hormone for maternal behavior in the mammal? *Hormones and Behavior,* 1971, *2,* 343–354.

4 Feeding Ecology and Mother-Infant Relations

Leonard A. Rosenblum
Gayle Sunderland
State University of New York at Brooklyn, N.Y.

With their interest in the evolution and phylogeny of behavioral adaptations, however, ecologists have until now paid little or no attention to the ontogeny of behavior. In the ecology of most animal species, the behavioral variables given most attention tend to be the species-characteristic behaviors of adults . . . .Human ecology therefore has to come to terms with ontogenetic development as one of the basic "processes" which determine the nature of adaptive capacities in human communities, populations, and groups. In addition, insofar as the nature of adult social motivations and needs are shaped during child development, any attempt to understand or exert control over adult social interactions for ecological purposes, must take this fact into account.
—[Ambrose, 1977, p. 5]

In the last 20 years we have learned a great deal indeed regarding many aspects of mother–infant relations in primates. We currently have available in varying degrees of abundance and clarity information regarding this primary relationship in at least 38 different species ranging across the primate order, studied under either field or laboratory conditions, and in some, but all too infrequent, instances in both types of settings. The range of laboratory work includes "normative" behavioral observations of mothers and infants living in social groups, single dyads living alone, infants reared with artificial mothers, infants reared without mothers at all either in total isolation or with peers (e.g., Harlow, 1958; Hinde, 1971; Rosenblum, 1971; Sackett, Holm, Rupenthal, & Farhrenbruch, 1976), and a large number of studies focusing on the effects of disrupting the ongoing mother–infant relationship once it has been established under one circumstance or another. (See Mineka & Suomi, 1978, for a recent review).

Although it now appears clear that peer contact (Harlow, 1969; Rosenblum, Coe, & Bromley, 1975) and relationships with other adults (Rosenblum, 1971; Dolhinow, 1978; Rosenblum & Kaufman, 1967) may in part substitute for or complement the infant's relationship with mother, there is general agreement that the primate infant begins life with an intense and relatively prolonged interactive relationship with the mother that is crucial to its survival. What is of particular concern to us in the present context is that in addition to the obvious role of mother in initially providing nutritional support and a haven of safety for the young infant, the mother has been identified as the primary (but not the single) socializing agent of the developing infant, "its first examplar of what the larger world is like" (Mason, 1978; Poirier, 1968; Rosenblum & Alpert, 1977). This socialization process initially centered around the mother is generally viewed as the pattern of experiences in the infant and juvenile period that fits the developing young into the structure of the adult social groups within which the infant and its mother function. It is at this point that we find an inordinate gap in our emerging knowledge. The exhaustive range of studies of wild primates now available make it clear that no single adult pattern may be viewed as uniformly characteristic of a species. Rather even the most essential dimensions of social structure (e.g., size and dispersion of groups, male–female ratios, hierarchical patterns, and forms of peer interactions in the young) appear to vary as a function of key environmental conditions within which particular groups are found (Altmann, 1974; Baldwin & Baldwin, 1976; Crook & Gartlan, 1966; Eisenberg, Mockenhirn & Rudran, 1972; Rowell, Din & Omar, 1968). Although phylogenetic variables play a very significant role in determining behavioral expression (Bernstein, 1971; Chalmers, 1973; Hainsworth & Wolf, 1979) cross-species comparisons of basic social elements have suggested that, at least for some sociality measures, more variance may be attributable to ecological than to phylogenetic factors (Spuhler & Jorche, 1975; see also Berry, 1977; Rosenblum, 1979).

On both empirical and theoretical grounds the single most frequently cited dimension of the environment that is viewed as affecting social structure to the greatest extent is the availability of food, its relative abundance, and its distribution in space and time (previous references and Clutton-Brock, 1975, 1977; Coelho, Bramblett, & Quick, 1977; Dittus, 1974; Gartlan, 1974; Izawa, 1978; Kummer, 1968; Richard, 1977). Despite this enormous growth in our understanding of the socioecology of primates and the simultaneously developing view (expressed here for humans) that "it is the function of any socialization process [in our terms the mother–infant relationship] to produce an organism that is adapted to its specific surroundings [Lewis & Freedle, 1977, p. 276]," we are struck by the following: Field studies have paid little direct attention to the impact of diverse feeding ecologies on differences in the mother–infant relationship within species and the processes through which the infant is socialized differently in different environments; and laboratory studies except for the gross environmental manipulations exemplified by isolation rearing have, with several notable exceptions, provided little information on the way in which the mother-infant relationship may mediate the effects of varying energetic (i.e., food) demands of the environment in the course of the socialization process.

It is relevant to note here that these limitations in the current body of knowledge regarding nonhuman primates speak directly to the potential usefulness of these animals as models through which further understanding at the human level can be attained. Life in a world community so disparate in the extremity and diversity of its environmental demands requires us to marshall data on every level of inquiry that might explicate the factors that alter, facilitate, or hinder infant development in these settings.

Although food availability and the requirements for its acquisition are crucial in many societies or social groups, the relevance of the work on the primate socioecology of feeding for human behavioral development falls within a broader context relating to the impact of varied environmental demands on mother-infant relations and infant development. In the U.S., for example, some 45% of single mothers with children 0-3 years of age work outside the home, and over 30% of married women with infants also work, nearly 80% engaging in full-time employment (Lamb, Suomi, & Stephenson, 1979). Current research and theory has suggested, however, that gross classification of developmental environments in terms of "working" or "nonworking" mothers, or in terms of social class distinctions, obscures rather than clarifies the actual forces operating to shape development. On the contrary, what is beginning to emerge from both intracultural and intercultural studies of human child care patterns and from animal studies is the adaptive nature of the mother-infant interactional process. A basic objective of this adaptive process is the construction of maternal "strategies," which take into account environmental demands and available resources for meeting these demands so as to maximize survival, health, and later adult functioning of the infant now in the mother's care as well as that of potential future offspring (Konner, 1977; Levine, 1977). Indeed, Lewis and Freedle (1977) have suggested that "social class differences reside in the strategy that parents adopt in socializing their children [p. 212]." These interactional perspectives then, focus our attention on specific functional aspects of behavior within particular, denotatively referenced settings, rather than on potentially arbitrary classificatory independent variables.

In studies of traditional non-Western societies when such factors as economic status, availability of schools for older children in families with young infants, and transitional family structure (e.g., changes from polygamous to monogamous households) within a single rural community are taken into account, consistent distinct patterns of mother-infant interaction emerge, evidently related to these environmental variables *within* a small, apparently homogeneous group (e.g., Leiderman & Leiderman, 1977). Similarly, socioeconomic status group comparisons within Western societies have assumed class homogeneity, which is often not warranted. Within designated social classes, notable differences in child care practices and attitudes (as well as measurable child development indices) can be found when such factors as social network, ethnicity, family size, and relative disorganization of community and family structure are controlled (Golden & Birns, 1969; Pavenstadt, 1965). Thus the range and effectiveness of parental strategies reflect the total environmental system, not merely a single, however salient, component. As an example, Leiderman and Leiderman (1977) in a study of three economic groups within a traditional community in Africa found that whereas all mothers worked in the fields and maintained close physical contact with their infants through at least 1 year of breast feeding, the nature of the mother–infant relationship differed according to specific measures of economic status such as size of farm and access to fuel and the local water supply; this was particularly true when status affected the direct demands on the mothers' time as well as her opportunity to send the older children in the family to school. In the families with the highest and lowest economic status the mothers spent less time in close contact with their infants than did mothers in the middle-income group. The high economic status group could send their older children to school but could afford to hire other young girls in the community to fill the infant caretaker role, traditionally filled by daughters over the age of 7. The lowest economic status group could not send older offspring to school, and so had available the infant's siblings to help provide care (e.g., watching the child in the fields while mother worked there or bringing the infant to the mother for nursing as she worked throughout the day). The middle economic group did send their older children to school but could not afford to hire a caretaker, so the mothers in this group carried their infants more and otherwise kept them in close proximity while working in the fields. In addition when comparing type of mother–infant interaction among these groups, it was found that the middle- and lower-status groups resembled each other most in spending the greater percentage of the time with their infants in utilitarian, caretaking tasks; this was in contrast to the greater percentage of contact time in the high-income group spent by mothers playing with and socially interacting with their infants. Although the lower-income group had older children to assist with their infants, they had more physical labor to perform in maintenance of the house; the assistance in child care given to high-income mothers allowed them to be free to spend more time with their infants in verbal and play interaction, a situation facilitated further by the fact that they had more convenient water and fuel which did not require the long daily walking trips to carry these supplies back to the home as was the case with low-income mothers. Thus this type of detailed analysis of a traditional rural community makes it clear that actual differences related to responsivity to environmental demands as experienced by a mother and her child may be lost if only a single aspect of the environment is taken into consideration (for example, the fact that in a traditional African agricultural community every mother does physical labor in her field).

It follows therefore that if we are to understand the impact of any primary environmental variable, including feeding demand, on the course of maternal behavior and infant development, detailed, contextually rich data must be obtained. In the material that follows, we attempt to describe an empirically based conceptual framework derived from field and laboratory data on various forms within which study of the relationship of feeding ecology and maternal-infant dyad patterning may be approached. The chapter goes on to present a description of the findings of our initial experimental efforts in this context, involving the study of foraging demand and mother-infant relations in the bonnet macaque.

OPTIMAL FORAGING THEORY

It is appropriate to begin this section with a brief consideration of the broad theories that have been developed regarding foraging behavior. From data of a number of species including mammals, birds, and fishes (e.g., MacArthur & Pianka, 1966), theories of optimal foraging strategy have been developed (Pyke, Pulliam & Charnov, 1977; Schoener, 1971). As the term *optimal* implies, these theories view foraging behavior as part of the total survival strategy of animals under various conditions in which there is a "trade-off" between attempts to maximize certain elements, for example, energy acquisition, and minimize other elements, for example, predators or plant toxins. Although optimization can be investigated for individual foragers (as is pertinent in some species), part of the equation of optimization involves the patterns of association and interaction with conspecifics, and it has been via this dimension that socioecological theorists have attempted to understand the relationship between feeding ecology and primate social structure. A significant aspect of current optimization theory regarding possible laboratory testing in a given group should shift with changing conditions (Pyke et al., 1977). Indeed, Fairbanks and Bird (1978) have recently shown that systematic differences emerge in interindividual distances in foraging patterns as the same groups of vervets forage through areas varying in cover (predation threat) and food abundance. Similarly despite preferred feeding locations species will often shift from terrestrial to arboreal feeding (e.g., toque macaques, Dittus, 1974) or vice versa (e.g., proboscis monkey, Kawabe & Mano, 1972) depending on immediate food availability.

Somewhat longer cyclic shifts in foraging patterns are also seen in many primates as climatic shifts from wet to dry seasons occur, with their resultant changes in the type and abundance of food supplies. Thus when seasonal shifts occur and food supplies dwindle, primate groups may: (1) begin to forage earlier in the day (e.g., baboons, Davidge, 1978); (2) change meal patterns (e.g.,

Propithecus, Richard, 1974; capuchins, Freese, 1978; *Callicebus,* Kinzey, 1977; see also discussion of meal patterns below); (3) increase home range; or (4) break up into smaller foraging groups and show less specialization in their food preferences (Clutton-Brock, 1977; Eisenberg et al., 1972; Gartlan, 1974; Kummer, 1968).

FEEDING AND AGGRESSION

A most significant element in the growing awareness of the importance of feeding in regulating primate social behavior is the fact that it is during feeding episodes that most agonistic behavior emerges within natural monkey groups (e.g., langur, Hrdy, 1977; lemur, Sussman, 1977; *Ateles,* Klein & Klein, 1977; toque macaque, Dittus, 1974; mangabeys, Chalmers, 1968; Japanese macaque, Izawa, 1978; bonnet macaque, Rahaman & Parthasarathy, 1969). Even in siamang and gorilla, in which overt aggression is relatively infrequent, mutual avoidance emerges and individual distances between subjects enlarge to their greatest extent during feeding (Chivers, 1977; Fossey & Harcourt, 1977).

The relative increase in competitive and agonistic behaviors during feeding does not appear to be a simple function of total food abundance, however, but rather may reflect adaptive responses to the relative dispersal of the available food (Altmann, 1974; Struhsaker & Leland, 1979). Thus in mangabey and chimps, for example, most fighting occurs over items such as large pieces of fruit or containerized food rather than dispersed food particles (Chalmers, 1968; Wrangham, 1974). Similarly, Southwick (1967), studying artificial feeding of free-ranging rhesus groups in India, demonstrated less aggression when the same amount of food was widely scattered as compared to equally abundant food offered in a single limited space; the same was true when seeds and rice were scattered as opposed to the presentation of a few large food items (Southwick, Siddiqi, Farooqui, & Pal, 1976).

In humans the effect of severe food deprivation on personal behavior and the dissolution of traditional affiliative societal activities is dramatically illustrated by the following description of a group of South American hunters who live on a near-starvation subsistence diet (Holmberg, cited in Bronfenbrenner, 1966):

> The evidence for strong appetitive and anxiety responses toward food in Siriono society is overwhelming. Behavior of this group is characterized by hasty preparation of food, lack of complex recipes, absence of standardized routines of eating, stealing off into the forest to eat, wolfing food, overeating, reluctance to share food, lack of food preferences except on a quantitative basis, absence of etiquette and ritual with respect to food, eating when sick, eating when not hungry, excessive quarreling over food, etc. [pp. 703].

This example of response to extreme environmental demand is illustrative of behavior under unusually harsh conditions that border on below-minimum requirements for survival and the ability of a social group to function cohesively. It reflects thereby, one end of the range of variability of human behavior in coping with demands imposed by the physical environment.

Before closing this section on feeding and aggressive behavior it is worth noting that in several observations of large troops of rhesus monkeys (Loy, 1970; Marsden, 1972; Southwick, 1967) relatively severe food deprivation resulted in a diminution of various forms of social behavior including overt aggression, and relatively lethargic, prolonged foraging activity. From a developmental standpoint it is also worth noting that such severe deprivation of food also resulted in dramatic decreases in infant and juvenile play behavior, a finding also corroborated by Baldwin and Baldwin (1976) for a natural group of squirrel monkeys observed in extremely unusual conditions of natural food scarcity.

HIERARCHICAL RELATIONS, MOTHER-INFANT INTERACTION, AND INFANT DEVELOPMENT

In order that we now bring those facts and theories regarding primate social structure, feeding adaptations, and related agonism into a developmental context, three issues need to be considered: First, that the hierarchical elements, which emerge during foraging and feeding, do in fact mediate different patterns of more or less successful foraging and related behaviors in animals that emerge as dominant or subordinate in these encounters; secondly, that in many species early infant environmental feeding appears in the context of the infant's close association with mother; and third, that in the course of early development, the mother through her support, interaction, and mere presence conveys aspects of her own rank to her offspring, which in turn influences the subsequent development of the infant's social behavior.

FORAGING AND HIERARCHICAL RELATIONS

It is true as Rowell (1974) has stated that within stable primate groups overt assertion of "dominance" is less frequent than more subtle or overt demonstrations of acquiescence and subordinance. This phenomenon may also be evidenced during foraging behavior, such that the demonstrable aggression described previously, although clearly of significance, may be more reflective of the failure of the usual subordinance patterns to function appropriately than the continuing need of higher-status animals to impose themselves on others. Thus Dittus (1977) in a recent account of foraging and dominance in toque macaques states:

> Dominant animals consistently fed, to the exclusion of subordinates, in the regions
> of the fruiting trees where fruit was ripest and most abundant. Subordinate animals

in addition to having their foods usurped generally avoided these "rich" areas where the dominants were feeding, and instead fed at poorer areas, or on different foods [p. 305].

Beginning with the early laboratory work on primate dominance-subordinance, priority access to food has been used as a consistent reflection of status in numerous species (Maslow, 1936), even in juvenile subjects (Warren & Maroney, 1958). The observations described earlier regarding agonism and feeding reflect similar rank-related outcomes between members of wild troops. Although not perfectly correlated (Bernstein, 1971) higher-status subjects, that is, those who "win" in agonistic encounters, tend to have greater access to available food and access to the most desired food and as a consequence may be viewed as demonstrating more efficient (i.e., the ratio of energy spent to energy obtained) foraging than lower-status subjects. Indeed as some workers have suggested, hierarchical patterns outside the feeding situation, in addition to allowing greater access to mates, may represent the group's preparedness for intermittent crises in food availability (Altmann, 1974; Dittus, 1974, 1977;Hrdy, 1977; Kummer, 1968; Plotnik, King, & Rogers, 1968; Pyke et al., 1977; Wilson, 1975).

STATUS AND MOTHER–INFANT RELATIONS AND KINSHIP

It is clear furthermore that in those contexts within which hierarchical behavior emerges most strongly, mothers' ranks are transmitted to their infants (e.g., rhesus: Koford, 1963; Marsden, 1968; Sade, 1965; baboons: Ransom & Rowell, 1972: langurs: Poirier, 1977; chimps: deWaal, 1978). In keeping with these earlier reports but focusing on still needed observations of the process of conferring rank on offspring, Cheney (1977) in a recent paper on rank acquisition during development notes that, "maternal aids of offspring appeared to be the major factor in determining the acquisition of rank among juveniles and subadults. ...Although all mothers aided their offspring, the offspring of high-ranking adult females were aided at a higher rate when they were threatened or attacked, than were the offspring of low-ranking females [p. 305]." Furthermore it is now reasonable to suggest that the entire social network of play and grooming relationships, for example, of the offspring of higher-status females, may be markedly different from that of offspring of low-status females. Thus, dominant female offspring are groomed and sought after more (Cheney, 1977, 1978; Seyfarth, 1977) by other adults and juveniles and engage in more social play amongst themselves and with others (Dittus, 1974; Fady, 1969; Fedigan, 1972; Gard & Meier, 1977; Poirier, 1977). Moreover, some of these studies suggest that through the coalescence of a number of these social interaction preferences, the offspring of more dominant females form more cohesive consanguinal family units than those of subordinates, thus facilitating the continuity of status across generations (Cheney, 1977; Fady, 1969; Seyfarth, 1977; see also Hinde, 1971; Rosenblum, 1971).

An additional point is worth noting here regarding the continuity of the mother-offspring bond. It would appear that kinship grouping does more than provide status support in dominant units. During food crises, heightened affiliative behavior within kinship groups, together with decreased nonkin interaction levels, suggests that kinship support may go beyond that of mere dominance status (Loy, 1970). Similarly the recent rather astonishing findings of Wu and Holmes (in press), indicating that pigtail young respond preferentially to half-siblings whom they have never seen before, further emphasizes our need to attend to variations in the functions of kinship structures within the large primate troops we study within varied socioecological contexts (see also Hinde, 1971; Rosenblum, 1971).

DEVELOPMENT OF INFANT FEEDING

When we add one additional element to this picture, we see further the importance of the feeding ecology-social-mother-infant chain in our attempt to understand the various paths of socialization in higher primates. In every species in which even the most fragmentary observations are presented, in keeping with the intense early bond of mothers and infants in primates, infants' initial attempts at nonlactate feeding occur in the close presence of the mother. In some species, infants begin by eating food scraps directly from the mother's mouth (e.g., patas, Hall, 1968; langurs, Poirier, 1977; orangs, Horr, 1977; galago, Charles-Dominique, 1977) and in many species infants begin eating at the mother's side, taking the same food she does (e.g., Japanese macaques, Azuma, 1973; Fedigan & Fedigan, 1977; Izawa, 1978; toque macaques, Dittus, 1974; De Brazza's monkey, Stevenson, 1973; langurs, Poirier, 1969; bonnet and pigtail macaques and squirrel monkeys, Rosenblum, personal observations). Although it should be noted that infant and particularly juvenile primates, albeit perhaps more than lower mammals (Bekoff, 1977), do not acquire all feeding habits by following the mother's behavior and may take feeding initiatives on their own (Frisch, 1968; Rhine & Westlund, 1978), nonetheless, according to Hinde (1971), "it is clear that infants learn a great deal from their mothers, especially in the context of avoidance and food getting behavior" [p. 32].

It is interesting to note that the capacity of human infants to focus behavior on stimuli toward which the mother's behavior is directed emerges early. Human infants show clear readiness and ability to follow the pointing behavior of their mothers by 14 months (Murphy & Messer, 1971), and it is clear that throughout the primate order, including humans, the feeding situation is among the most significant contexts within which the early mother–infant relationship functions (cf. Lewis & Goldberg, 1969; Martin, 1975).

WEANING

A most significant additional perspective should be appended here, that is, factors that potentially influence the point at which major energy expenditures made by the mother on behalf of the infant can be expected to be reduced or withdrawn. Though the variations in the age of infant independence (including completed weaning) are generally enacted within phylogenetic variations, (Chalmers, 1968; Struhsaker & Leland, 1979; Sussman, 1977), there is reason to consider the likelihood that ecological pressures may be reflected in intraspecific variations as well. Thus in the only observation directly addressing this point we have been able to find, Gartlan and Brain (1968) noted that in an area of "impoverished and deteriorating" resources as compared to one that was "rich and regenerating," observations of *Cercopithecus aethiops* dyads indicated that in the poor area, where the group dispersed some distance to feed, "the mother infant bond seemed more intense." These authors also suggest that "the long-term results of strong interanimal bonds in an environment such as this (where the group is often physically dispersed) are probably of great adaptive significance [p. 271]." This finding fits with those obtained under more acute deprivation conditions in macaques (Loy, 1970; Rosenblum, Kaufman & Stynes, 1969). However one must also consider in this context the significant theoretical contribution of Trivers (1974) regarding weaning conflict in animals. In essence the Trivers hypothesis, employing Hamilton's concepts of inclusive fitness, suggests that parental investment in young should be withdrawn at the point at which (reproductive) cost to the mother (in this case) exceeds the (reproductive) benefit to the offspring or in other words at the point at which the mother, in terms of the likelihood of passing along her genetic traits, has more to lose than gain in the continued support of her current young. The infant, whose investment in passing along its own genetic material is generally greater than that of the mother, may resist to varying degrees the attempted withdrawal of parental investment. This disparity of interest, perhaps enhanced in poor ecological settings in which the mother has difficulty replenishing her energy supplies and the infant has difficulty obtaining its own supplies directly emerges as the "weaning conflict."

Although, as alluded to previously, the rate of attaining independence differs widely in many species of primates both within and across broad feeding ecology groups, one would expect that varying resources within a given species, along with all the other factors we have described, should result in alterations in time-to-weaning. As Trivers has suggested, one might expect such factors as species, size (and relative state of maturation) of infants at time of scarcity, replenishment rate of energy resources in the environment, and their dispersal (and hence procurement costs), all to have considerable influence on the potential withdrawal of parental care. Although we know from several species that times of hardship result in increased infant and juvenile mortality but not decreases in reproductive rate (Dittus, 1977; Eisenberg et al., 1972; Struhsaker & Leland, 1979), at present that is all we know. Except for the observations of Gartlan and Brain, cited earlier, and these mortality data, little is known of the dynamic impact on the developing mother–infant relationship when the foraging demand of the environment is altered during a significant portion of the infant's early life.

Data on humans suggests that one of the unfortunate effects which heightened environmental demands can have on a parent is that of attenuating nurturant maternal behavior. As in Gelles' study of child abuse (1974) child neglect has been related to low SES and, more specifically, environmental stress within low-income groups (Giovannoni & Billingsly, 1971). In the latter study parental adequacy in low-income families of three ethnic backgrounds was assessed, and it was found that neglect was associated with high environmental stress (e.g., large number of children in the family, single parent family) and more clearly related to immediate situational effects rather than being dependent on the mother's history. As in the case of child abuse, the effects of the environment on parental adequacy are mediated by individual characteristics, but a highly stressful, precarious living situation will elicit pathological coping behavior in parents who in a more stable, supportive setting would be able to function fairly adequately.

On a less dramatic level, and perhaps in more direct relation to the nonhuman data on withdrawal or diminution of parental investment, Katz (1970) has suggested that in some lower-class, more stress-laden groups there is more social and emotional distance between parents and children, earlier relaxation of close parental supervision, and more children who are precociously independent of adult influence and excessively influenced by peers. Similarly Wallston (1971) also found that the child of a working mother can be more assertive and independent than the child of a nonworking mother, provided that he or she receives stable care.

Furthermore in light of current sociobiological perspectives regarding parental investment in individual infant survival, it is worth noting that in considering the impact of parental stress and environmental factors on long-term effects of perinatal distress, Sameroff (1976) has proposed a "caretaking casualty continuum." In a study addressing this issue it was found that the long-term effects of perinatal distress, (e.g., anoxia, problem delivery) were mediated by SES, family stability, and mother's IQ and education; the significance of SES seemed to lie in its relationship to the degree of stress, deprivation, and lack of education experienced by the mother, which in turn influenced the mother–infant interaction. In other words, the effects of social status (in conjunction with attendant personal and environmental factors) could reduce or amplify intellectual deficits related to perinatal trauma; caretaking by deprived, stressed, and poorly educated parents exacerbated early difficulties.

In general as we gather increasing data on human development and parental roles, as Herzog and Lewis (1971) point out, the "culprit variable" approach in looking at environmental and parental impact on child development is giving way to an interaction model where individual characteristics of mothers, children, and family situation are considered in conjunction with more traditional "environmental" variables such as SES. These authors emphasize the importance of the mediation of the stressful environment of poor families by quality of mothering; the effects of maternal employment outside the home on children varies considerably according to such factors as mother's temperament, family stability, and a variety of other relevant stress factors.

To return to the perspective provided by the animal data described earlier, we are able to sketch in the following picture: The infant begins to explore and feed at its mother's side quite early, accompanies her during her own foraging and feeding-related status encounters, and gradually acquires to a significant degree both her feeding preferences and patterns of food access. In conjunction with complementary patterns of interaction during nonfeeding periods, the primate young emerges from the infant period (i.e., by the end of year 1 in many species) a functioning component in the social–feeding ecology nexus.

To conclude this section we may then summarize the existing data as follows: (1) Feeding ecology is viewed as a key determinant of primate social structure both in terms of relatively long-term and more acute strategic responses to changing environmental demands; (2) foraging is the setting in most species within which hierarchical behaviors are most apparent; the more competitive the feeding situation, the more dominance–subordinance agonism, and status-related issues are in evidence; (3) mothers actively attempt to convey their status to offspring; and (4) as a consequence of these converging factors the infant joins the social group in reflecting in its social- and object-directed behaviors the adaptive demands of the ecological setting they all share.

LABORATORY RESEARCH

As we turn our attention from the field to the laboratory, we find that the lines of evidence linking feeding patterns to meaningful alterations in mother–infant relationships are tenuous. To be sure, a limited number of studies have manipulated nonfeeding aspects of the environment while assessing mother–infant relations. These require our attention because they reflect the fact that the mother–infant relationship in primates is indeed malleable in many species and can reflect meaningful differences in the physical and social environment in which they function. At the grossest level, for example, several reports suggest that significant changes in mother-infant relations occur when subjects are observed in "cage" versus "wild" settings. These differences, as is perhaps true of all such environmentally based variations, do not generally reflect changes in the total behavioral repertoire but rather the frequency of occurrence of various behaviors. Thus Rowell (1967) in observing baboons under both conditions, states: "The same units of social behavior were observed in both wild and caged populations, and no behavior patterns were seen in one and not the other [p. 499]." (See also Kummer & Kurt, 1965). There are similar reports for pigtail (Bernstein, 1970) and bonnet macaques (Parthasarathy, 1979). Nonetheless, compared to subjects in "the wild," baboon mothers in captivity apparently restrict their younger infants more (Nash, 1978; Rowell, 1967, 1968); similarly, captive chimpanzee mothers manipulate their infants more (Nicolson, 1977). Captive dyads in Japanese macaques (Itiogawa, 1973) and chimpanzees, on the other hand, reduce close contact appreciably earlier than their wild counterparts, in the case of chimps as much as 2 years earlier (Nicolson, 1977).

Environmental Influences on Mother-Infant Relations and Gender Differences

More focused, environmental manipulations have also demonstrated the adjusting capacity of the mother-infant relationship although the dynamics of that adjustment process are as yet unclear. For example, in an early series of reports, Jensen and his colleagues (Jensen, Bobbitt & Gordon, 1968, 1969) studied pigtail macaque dyads under several environmental conditions during the first 15 weeks of life. When single dyads were compared in a "rich" versus "privation" cage (despite the fact that both settings in retrospect seem quite barren), infants in the relatively richer environment were more independent of their mothers at an earlier age, apparently as a result of their own initiative towards independence rather than as a result of any change in maternal behavior. These data, despite the very restricted quality of the environmental manipulations, lead the authors to conclude "environment does not affect the basic nature of the mother's role." In a later study from the Jensen laboratory, (Wolfheim, Jensen, & Bobbitt, 1970) in which group-versus-individual caged (all female infants) were examined at 3-4 months, group infants were found to be less independent than single infants, and *this* social-environmental shift reflected more a change in maternal protectiveness than in infant fearfulness. Thus the relative contributions of changes in maternal and infant behavior in different settings remains unclear.

In an important refinement of some of their data analyses, that is, using sequence analyses, these authors determined that maternal rejection ("hitting") in the privation environment but not the rich setting, was more likely to induce the infant to separate; this effect however was primarily true for female infants. Such sex differences in response to the characteristics in varied environmental settings are (as we see later) of great importance and have been particularly implicated in studies of severe environmental deprivation (isolation) in which female primates fare far better than males (Sackett et al., 1976).

Based on these and related studies, several years ago the senior author suggested a model attempting to relate gross physical and social environmental complexity to the growth of infant independence in monkeys (Rosenblum, 1971). This age-dependent model suggested a changing relationship of environmental complexity to infant independence from one of little initial impact, to a U-shaped function during later infancy to an increasingly positive monotonic relationship by later adolescence. Although Nicolson (1977) in a recent review suggests that this early model fits most of the existing data, in its original form the model failed to take into account the crucial added dimension of gender differences in development. Thus in a test of this model (Rosenblum, 1974) in which squirrel monkey dyads were raised in two levels of social and physical environmental complexity in the first 4 weeks of life, no differences in dyadic contact across conditions or gender appeared from about 4–10 weeks, and infants of both genders were relatively less independent of their mothers in the more complex environment; however, after 12 weeks of age, male infants in the complex setting were significantly more independent, moving more freely away from mother, than either female in the same environment or males in the less complex setting. Females in the more complex environment maintained relatively heightened levels of contact with mother, lending support to one of the Jensen findings; these differences between environments were apparently due to differences in response of the male and female infants and not their respective mothers. It is interesting to note that when observed in one of their "natural habitats," that is, a small town, human male adolescents were determined to have more extensive "home-ranges" than girls of similar age (Moore & Young, 1978).

Other studies in our laboratory (Rosenblum, 1978; Rosenblum, Coe, & Bromley, 1975; Rosenblum & Plimpton, 1979) have confirmed the range of important sex differences in infant responses to mothers and others in varying environmental settings. Thus, for example, in systematic apparatus testing of group-reared bonnet macaque infants, males show less preferential response to mothers and more readiness to approach conspecific strangers than females. When infants are reared with mothers alone however, both male and female infants show virtually no differentiation of response to mothers and strangers even as late as 8 months of age (Rosenblum & Alpert, 1977). Although not addressed to gender differences, Kaplan (1972) has also observed rearing conditions effects on recognition and preferential response to conspecifics and has repeatedly implicated species, sex, and environmental rearing condition in influencing this essential aspect of the infant monkey's selective relationship with mother. Relevant gender differences during early social development in both field and laboratory studies of primates have also been recorded in various other species (macaques, Dittus, 1974; Fady, 1969; Itiogawa, 1973; Mitchell, 1968; baboons, Cheney,

1977, 1978; and chimpanzees, deWaal, 1978). Gender differences have also been given primary consideration regarding variations in primate group structure in terms of longer-term offspring–mother relationships and their dissolution in numerous species (e.g., Gartlan, 1974; Kummer, 1968; Struhsaker & Leland, 1979).

Food Deprivation Studies

In keeping with the "starvation" data presented above, rhesus macaque and squirrel monkey infants maintained under sustained low-protein diets have been observed to be relatively inactive, seem preoccupied with the food that is available, are less curious and playful, and show heightened xenophobia (Chappell, 1977; Zimmerman, Geist, & Ackles, 1975). Paralleling the suggestion of Gartlan and Brain, cited earlier, in a limited study of mother–infant relations in rhesus monkeys, Slocum and Strobel (1976) in a brief account indicate that the single low-protein mother of their study "allowed her infant less freedom ... seemed more anxious ... clung to her infant more, and spent more time in bodily contact with the infant." Of course, as in the studies of human malnutrition (e.g., Ricciuti, 1977), a variety of other environmental and social factors make interpretation of such limited food-deprivation data difficult, but the suggestion of the Slocum and Strobel study was that the primary impact of undernutrition was on the mothers' behavior, at least during the first 6 months of the infants' lives.

In a comparative study of bonnet and pigtail macaques we did some years ago (Rosenblum, et al., 1969) an interesting pattern of response to acute food deprivation was obtained. Observations were carried out around the clock, and 48 hours of food deprivation was periodically instituted. As a result a series of changes of dyadic and adult behavior was observed at various times of day in pigtails, but a similar bonnet group showed little dramatic effect. During deprivation yearling pigtails showed significant increases in contact with their mothers during daylight hours and a diminution of play with peers; bonnet infants of comparable age showed neither effect. (Gender effects were not assessed). Similarly only pigtail adults showed significant decreases in social grooming. This perhaps reflected both the heightened levels of foraging behavior in this group at several times of day as well as some increases in group tension, which is generally higher in laboratory groups of pigtails than bonnets. (See also Bronfenbrenner, 1966). However, with regard to the latter point, it should be noted that characteristic levels of proximity and physical contact between adults were not changed in either species nor were the usually low levels of overt aggression seen in these stable groups. It is important furthermore that the increased dyadic contact in pigtails occurred despite the fact that infants were a year or more of age, well after major developmental reductions in daytime contact patterns had occurred. Thus even these older dyadic units adjusted to abrupt changes in feeding level although species effects and diurnal variations in these effects were markedly in evidence.

Food Procurement Studies

There have been some efforts in laboratory settings to determine the effects of difficulty in food procurement on feeding and related behavior. When adequate nutrition is maintained, the introduction of some form of special apparatus or operant device that must be worked upon for some period of time to obtain the normal day's ration produces quite interesting results. Following an aborted early effort by Ferster, Hammer, and Randolph (1968) to maintain chimps in a totally operant-controlled environment, Murphy (1976) has recently demonstrated that simply requiring zoo-living chimps and orangs to manipulate a simple device to extract their food markedly reduced their prior levels of stereotypy and related "cage-neurosis behavior." Furthermore in these subjects imposition of even an FI-6 minute schedule led to a marked reduction in food wastage (most obtained food was eaten) as opposed to CRF conditions. Similarly Natelson and Bonbright (1978), studying individual rhesus living in a restricted operant chamber, has shown that even the introduction of an FR-3 schedule reduced food wastage and significantly reduced the number of spontaneous eating and drinking cycles each day compared to those recorded under CRF. Baldwin and Baldwin (1976) have also presented a most interesting laboratory follow-up to their observations of diminished play in a wild squirrel monkey troop in which food was scarce and foraging requirements were high. This lab study showed that requiring squirrel monkey juveniles to extricate their food from a complex hopper, or presenting food in powdered form, thus requiring increased food acquisition time and effort, resulted in very marked reduction in social play in these group living subjects; they conclude that "even minor changes in food ecology can reduce the frequency of play by half." Furthermore, they demonstrated that the more restricted the access to food, the greater was the impact on social play in these subjects.

Collier Simulations of Feeding Ecology

We now turn to a brief summary of the work of Collier and his associates on laboratory simulations of optimal foraging behavior (Collier, 1978; Collier & Rovee-Collier, 1980; Kanarek, 1976; Kaufman, Collier & Brashier, in press; Marwine & Collier, 1979) because of their effectiveness in demonstrating the efficacy of laboratory simulations of this type. Using a combination of operant methodology and a mixture of food-acquisition techniques, these workers have assessed the effects of varying energy–time requirements at each of three stages in the "feeding chain": food search (foraging), food procurement (acquirement once the food is "located") and actual food consumption. This approach, in one type of study, employs varying operant demands (e.g., FR1–FR5120) on a device that allows the animals access to a meal of whatever size it chooses whenever it chooses (24 hours per day). In keeping with optimal foraging models (e.g., Pyke et al., 1977; Schoener, 1971) these studies provide data on wild and laboratory rats, guinea pigs, chickens, ferrets, and cats, which indicate that when the energetic costs involved in the procurement of food goes up, the number of meals per day decreases, and the size of each meal increases. Variations on this method have also shown that when the animal is offered food of either high- or low-procurement cost (another operant schedule) at the end of a given "search," the greater the search costs, the greater the likelihood that the animal will take whatever meal opportunity is found, irrespective of procurement costs. This effect is clearly analogous to the decreased specialization in diet under different foraging conditions observed in the wild and diminished wastage data discussed earlier. Without going deeply into further details regarding the whole series of significant variables systematically identified in this seminal research program, several points are particularly relevant: There are marked species differences in the threshold of search costs at which animals change their meal-frequency-meal-size patterns; when procurement cost increases, only species that are *social feeders* increase their response rate during the procurement phase, a likely adaptation to competitive feeding situations; and finally, this research as a whole has emphasized our need to understand the ways in which variation in ecological demands at each level of the feeding chain can change the total effort towards optimization of feeding strategies in each species we study.

This rather multidimensional review of existing information on the social and developmental impact of environmental demands, in particular those which in human and nonhuman primates alter the total workload of caregiving figures, has led us to consider a new perspective within which to carry out our laboratory research on mother–infant relations in monkeys: the assessment of the chain of interacting events that encompasses feeding (i.e., foraging) requirements; concomitant alterations in group social patterns; adjustments in the character of the mother–infant interaction; and congruent alterations in the path of infant development toward adaptive functioning in environments of varied demands.

The remainder of this chapter presents our initial efforts towards this objective. But first it is necessary to apprise the reader of the basic requirements we feel it necessary to embody in the paradigm of differential foraging demands for group-living monkeys in a laboratory setting in order that evolutionary validity be maintained.

We established five basic objectives for our approach to this problem:

1. The technique must allow variations in required feeding-time budgets, search and/or procurement demands ranging from virtual ad-lib feeding to considerable time–energy feeding requirements; this must be possible while the physical structure of experimental environments remains relatively constant to avoid confounding influences of other environmental alterations. The setting

should however allow food acquisition to be well within the learning-performance capacity of all subjects, prior to the usual age of weaning in these animals (cf. Bernstein, 1971; Collier, 1978; Schoener, 1971).

2. The technique adopted should allow for variations in dispersal quality, that is, clumped, patchy, or dispersed supply at varying levels of abundance (cf. Altmann, 1974; Pyke et al., 1977; Southwick et al., 1976).

3. The means of acquiring food should allow for foraging either singly or in small subgroups of subjects; this is critical for example in allowing social affiliations and status factors to influence foraging patterns in the group; this is also crucial in allowing developing infants to forage with mother or separate from her (cf. Bekoff, 1977; Chalmers, 1968b; Eisenberg et al., 1972; Struhsaker & Leland, 1979).

4. The environment should allow feeding competition and displacement but prevent dominant subjects from complete control of food access as occurs in many laboratory food-competition test situations.

5. The task of food acquisition should require subjects to locomote through the environment to seek food; this element is an important aspect of natural costs and can allow emergence of foraging strategies of relevance, for example, "trap lining" (Charles-Dominique, 1977; Hainsworth & Wolf, 1979; see also Anderson, Kenney, & Mason, 1977, and Mason & Berkson, 1975, for the importance of maternal mobility and its relation to adequate infant development).

In an attempt to meet these essential requirements, we designed and built a series of identical foraging units. They were constructed of three panels of surplus, 2½-in. diamond-shaped iron mesh affixed to one another with their openings in line thus creating a large series of diamond-shaped channels; the mesh panels each measured approximately 4 ft. high and 7 ft. long. Attached to the rear panel were a series of galvanized iron troughs, running the long axis of the panels, and set with approximately 3-in. spaces between them (see Fig. 4.1). Standard Purina monkey chow crackers were placed in these troughs. When the whole unit was placed with the trough-containing panels against a wall, subjects could not see the food crackers but could readily reach through the mesh channels and, if food were located, could easily remove it (see Fig. 4.2 and 4.3).

Each unit of this type contained a series of food troughs and approximately 250 juxtaposed channels at which food crackers might be located; these channels ranged from floor level to about 4 ft. from the floor. Each living area was composed of a double pen of 120 sq. ft. (7 ft. high) whose opaque dividing wall contained one floor-level, pass-through door at its rear, and one similar door near the front ceiling; three levels of resting shelves were present at the rear of each half of the double pen. A foraging unit was placed along each long wall surface, that is, four units for each double pen. These four units afforded a total of approximately 1000 potential food loci. Automatic watering spouts were con-

FIG. 4.1   The two mesh-covered foraging panels and a mother carrying two pieces of food just recovered from a panel.

FIG. 4.2.   Adult female attempting visual search of the foraging panel.

FIG. 4.3.   Adult female, with one piece of food in her cheek-pouch, manually checking another potential site.

tinuously available in each half-pen. Observations were carried out through one-way–vision mirrors in the front wall of each pen.

With this arrangement subjects could move freely between the various units, as part of a foraging strategy, or if displaced from one while foraging could shift to another unit on the same side or to the adjacent pen; no single subject could maintain control of this total foraging environment. Acquisition of food, once located, was simple and readily accomplished by all adult subjects on their first attempts; infants easily retrieved food by 3 months of age (see Fig. 4.4).

It should be noted that many other approaches to this problem were also considered. For example, several operant levers could have been used thus allowing considerable flexibility in schedules of reinforcement available at each lever. However we felt strongly that such devices would inhibit locomotion (an important segment of natural foraging costs), prevent most patterns of social foraging to emerge (including mother–infant dyadic patterns), and potentially allow more dominance control of access unless other severe restrictions on sociality were imposed. Similarly more complex manipulanda could have been used (e.g., puzzle-boxes, doors and latches to be opened) as a means of increasing procurement time; but preliminary efforts suggested that environmental maintenance problems would be severe; and unless such devices automatically reset themselves, a site, once checked by an animal would signal its emptiness to all others thus effectively reducing overall foraging demand as the day progressed.

FIG. 4.4.   A four-month-old infant searching for food at a foraging panel. Note mother and her infant entering through the rear pass-through door.

Subjects.   The subjects of this study were 10 bonnet macaque females and their respective offspring, split into two roughly age-matched (for offspring) groups of 5 dyads per group, each with 3 males and 2 female infants. Offspring ranged from 6 to 17 weeks at the start of the experiment and one infant was born 7 weeks into the study. (The data following exclude the youngest infants of each group).

Procedure.   One group was designated the low–foraging–demand (LFD) and one the high–foraging-demand (HFD) group. Each lived in an identical double pen. Except on weekends (discussed later) each foraging unit was checked and loaded every morning at 8:30 a.m. (1 hour after "lights-on"). Because, it must be emphasized, *this was not a study of food deprivation,* adequate food was provided for both groups; based on past experience with these types of subjects, their body weights, and lactational status (lactating females require about 25% more calories than cycling females [Coelho et al., 1977]) approximately 90–100 crackers were present in the HFD group's units and approximately 600 crackers were present at the start of each day in the LFD units.

Because there was little background data on health maintenance in these foraging regimes and bearing in mind the fact that under ad-lib feeding conditions, some bonnets have a tendency toward overeating and obesity (Rosenblum

& Smiley, 1980) weekend feedings in both the HFD and LFD groups was supplemented with several extra pans of laboratory chow, to be sure that all adult subjects of each group essentially maintained their prestudy body weights.

Observations.   After 2 weeks of acclimation to their new environments, 14 weeks of observation were carried out. Several types of observational routines were employed in this work. Two days per week, each infant, and on 2 other days, each mother, was observed for 10 minutes of focal animal, 10-second time-samples. These observations covered a range of mother–infant, social, self-, and foraging behaviors. Because dyadic interaction was recorded on both the infant and mother sheets, 40 minutes of observation per week were available for each mother–infant dyad. In addition to focal animal samples, at 8:30 a.m., 10:00 a.m., 1:00 p.m., and 4:00 p.m. each day, four spatial maps were completed across a 5–10 minute period, indicating the location of each subject throughout the double pen and their engagement in several social and foraging behaviors. Special observations have also included several around-the-clock records of foraging and related activities.

General Results.   For the 14 weeks of the study, health checks and weekly weight records indicated that subjects in both groups maintained excellent health; infants showed apparently normal weight gains. Subjects in the low-demand group (LFD) removed as much as 50% of the provided crackers each day, but generally discarded a very large portion (up to 50%) of the procured food (see Fig. 4.5). The subjects in the high-demand group (HFD), however, removed over 90% of provided food and consumed every piece that was found. Thus the negative relationship between foraging cost and "food specialization" recorded in the field and in other laboratory simulations appeared to operate in this situation as well.

The imposition of the two foraging demands produced a number of general differences in the adult–adult and mother–infant patterns in the two groups. The HFD group was generally more tense, less cohesive in terms of adult affiliative patterns of passive contact and social grooming, and more frequently engaged in hierarchically related behaviors in terms of such patterns as threatening, fighting, displacement, subordinate gestures, and flight. Not surprisingly, the adults of the HFD group engaged in appreciably more frequent foraging behavior with the apparatus, and this pattern, as predicted, seemed to provide the pivot around which social adjustments occurred. There was evidence as well that the infants of the HFD dyads appeared to function more independently of their mothers than did their age-matched counterparts in LFD.

Specific Findings.   As reflected in Fig. 4.6 hierarchical behaviors reflecting both dominance and subordinance appeared most frequently in the HFD group over the study period. After the first 4 weeks such behaviors were more

FIG. 4.5. A female of the LFD group inspecting some of the uneaten food removed from the foraging panels.

than twice as frequent in HFD as LFD; indeed in LFD two-thirds of the time individual subjects showed no hierarchical behavior for the entire week, whereas HFD subjects failed to engage in such encounters during only 36% of the weekly intervals.

As the same figure also illustrates foraging behavior was about five times higher in HFD than LFD, across the 14 weeks of the study. However one subject in HFD, the most subordinate female, virtually never engaged in foraging behavior at all; this female maintained herself successfully by avidly watching her partners forage and hastily grabbing any scraps of food dropped by them. Conversely, one female in LFD, who delivered her infant halfway into the study, had several periods of relatively high foraging prior to her parturition. The remaining four subjects of each group showed no overlap in their foraging scores, with these HFD subjects averaging 10 times as much foraging per week as those in the LFD group (12.0 vs. 1.2). Diurnal observations also indicated that although group differences were highest in the morning, after the panels were filled (the time when reinforcement ratios were highest) foraging was higher in HFD throughout the day. Similarly after lights-out LFD immediately ceased activity, whereas HFD continued to forage for an additional hour; neither group ever foraged more than 2 hours after lights were extinguished. The HFD group however began foraging immediately after lights were turned on again in the morn-

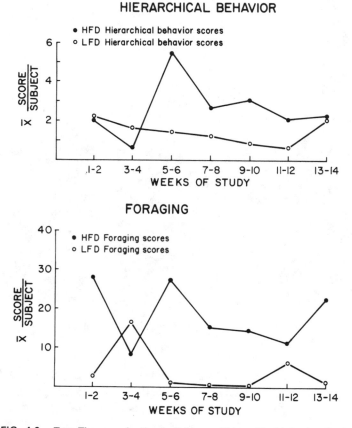

FIG. 4.6.   Top: The mean levels of all forms of hierarchical behaviors in the groups.

ing, whereas LFD generally did not begin their food-directed behavior until about 1½ hours later.

In addition to the general relationship of higher levels of foraging and hierarchical behaviors in HFD, there was some consistency in the week-to-week relationship of these two patterns as well. For the HFD group, hierarchical and foraging levels showed a positive .41 correlation (Pearson product-moment) across the 14 weeks of the study. It is worth noting here that the heightened levels of hierarchical behavior associated with the high foraging levels of HFD primarily centered around the foraging panels and resulted in relatively inefficient foraging behavior, particularly among the more subordinate group members. Subjects were often quite nervous while foraging, visually checking the location of partners and moving away from more dominant group members; as an apparent correlate of this tension, HFD subjects changed foraging panels and rooms frequently or would at times repeatedly check the same locations on a given panel after some social disruption had occurred. Indeed, despite the high total foraging levels we recorded in this group during our detailed observations, we could not discern the development of any straightforward, consistently maintained foraging strategy during the 14 weeks of the study. It is possible that more detailed analysis or more prolonged experience for these animals will provide the basis for the emergence and description of such strategies, but it would appear from these preliminary data that the levels of social tension we observed deterred their ready development.

As illustrated in Fig. 4.7 the high levels of HFD foraging and hierarchical behaviors were also reflected in their relatively low levels of adult affiliative behaviors, that is, adult contact and social grooming. Adult contact scores in LFD were nearly 80% higher, averaging 59.4 week, compared to 40.9 in HFD. The negative relationship between foraging demand and adult affiliation is best reflected in the strong negative correlation of $-.78$ on a weekly basis between foraging and adult contact scores in HFD. In a comparable fashion, weekly total grooming scores were also more than twice as high in LFD as HFD with average scores of 29.2 and 14.2 per subject in the two groups, respectively.

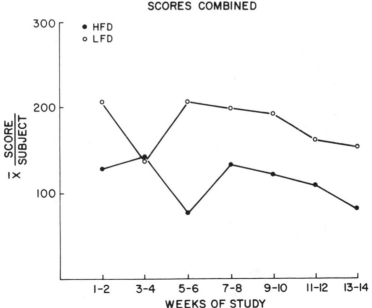

FIG. 4.7.   The mean levels of combined scores for adult–adult contact and adult–adult social grooming in the two groups.

Turning to the dyadic relationship of the mothers and their infants in the two groups, we were somewhat surprised to find that despite or perhaps because of the high tension levels in HFD, the infants in the high-demand group seemed more independent of their mothers than age counterparts in LFD. Figure 4.8 reflects the ratio of the time spent in dyadic contact (i.e., "contact" scores) to time spent with the two members of the dyad separated across the two pens, out of sight of one another, (i.e., "adjacency" scores).

The dyadic contact scores were relatively equivalent in the two groups; in the last month of the study, for example, they ran only slightly higher in LFD (mean score per subject per week = 30.6) than in HFD (mean = 25.6). Adjacency scores, on the other hand, were generally higher in the HFD infants throughout the study. Indeed each HFD infant had higher overall adjacency scores than its age counterpart in LFD, and in the last four weeks of the study the two groups

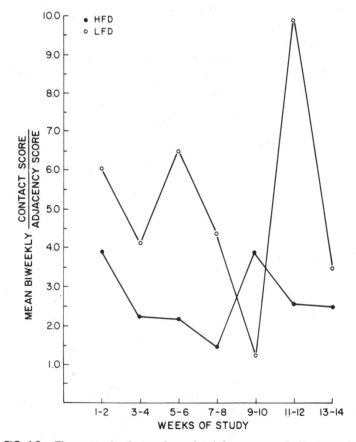

FIG. 4.8.   The mean ratio of scores for mother–infant contact and adjacent pen in the two groups.

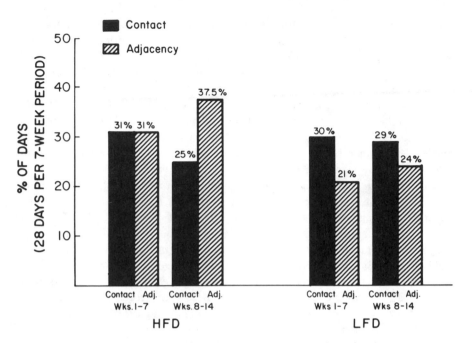

FIG. 4.9. The percentage of individual days in which members of each group met criterion levels of high-contact or high-adjacency in each half of the study period.

averaged 40.4 and 23.8 adjacency scores per subject, respectively. Daily contact scores greater than 80% of maximum possible, and adjacency scores greater than 20% of maximum possible, were used to estimate the days in which infants engaged in high levels of contact and/or high levels of adjacency. Figure 4.9 illustrates the proportions of days that infants in the two groups reached criterion levels in the first and last half of the study. HFD subjects showed an equal number of high contact and adjacency days in weeks 1–7 and an increased proportion of days spent in sustained separation from mother in the last 7 weeks; on the other hand, LFD infants, although engaging in an equal number of high contact days as infants in HFD, never showed as high a proportion of criterion adjacency days. Examinations of the duration of the individual excursions into adjacent pens in the two groups during the last 7 weeks of the study revealed this same fact in another way. Whereas 55–60% of all adjacency excursions in both groups lasted between 10–30 seconds, 20.4% of all HFD excursions lasted longer than 100 seconds, but LFD infants separated themselves from their mothers into the adjacent pens for such long periods on only 9.2% of all adjacency excursions.

It is important to note at this point that in both groups, infants initiated 60–64% of all adjacencies by moving through the connecting doors themselves;

furthermore infants were overwhelmingly the terminators of such separations accounting for 97–99% of all reunions of dyads following a period of adjacency. As one final note regarding the emerging independence of the infants in the two groups, rejection of the infants by their mothers was relatively infrequent and comparable in both groups as is typical of the bonnet mothers we observed throughout the years. This was particularly true with regard to punitive deterrence of contact and overt removal of the infant from contact; perhaps importantly, however, weaning of infants, after the first two weeks, was appreciably higher in HFD than LFD, averaging 6.0 per subject across the last 12 weeks in HFD and only 1.5 per subject in LFD.

One final point is worth noting in the data of this preliminary study of foraging demand. Despite the effectiveness of the imposed foraging demand and the apparent tensions in the HFD group, the frequency of social play observed amongst the infants of the two groups was in fact quite comparable across the entire study. This stands in rather marked contrast to the previous findings of Baldwin and Baldwin (1976) on the effects of feeding demands on play in squirrel monkeys. In the current study the infants showed average play scores of 12.8 and 12.2 in HFD and LFD in the first 7 weeks and scores of 11.0 and 14.2, respectively, in the final 7 weeks of the study. Although further analysis may reveal some additional differences in the last half of the study (e.g., three of the four infants in LFD played more than their HFD age-mates and the remaining pair was equal) it is clear that no dramatic differences in social play levels emerged as a function of the foraging demand.

Conclusions. What are the suggestive findings of this first experimental study of foraging demand effects on social and mother–infant patterns in nonhuman primates?

1. The foraging demand situation effectively met our stated requirements derived from the field data. Subjects successfully maintained themselves under both levels of demand. HFD subjects showed persistently high levels of foraging activity throughout the day, showing relatively longer foraging bouts, and were unspecialized in their selections, eating virtually all food obtained. LFD subjects foraged quickly and easily, devoting a small portion of their day to such activities and were extremely selective in eating the food procured. Infants were capable of executing the foraging task but engaged relatively infrequently in this activity. Except for a tendency toward high foraging levels in the morning when reinforcement rates were highest, no clearly systematic foraging techniques emerged.

2. In keeping with basic field data the higher foraging demand in HFD appeared to be correlated with an increased level of all types of hierarchical behavior centered around but not exclusively related to the foraging activity itself. Noteworthy however is the fact that these hierarchical behaviors

functioned smoothly, and neither injuries nor complete social disruption appeared. However as a further reflection of the different feeding requirements, HFD adults were less cohesive as a group, spending consistently less time in passive contact with one another and engaging in less social grooming than the subjects of the LFD group.

3. The mother–infant dyads were also influenced by the different foraging regimens. Infants of the HFD group functioned more autonomously than those in the LFD condition. Although physical contact scores and infant control of separations and returns were comparable in the two groups, HFD infants were more often separated from their mothers into adjacent pens and spent longer periods apart when separated. Some tendency toward more weaning by HFD mothers appeared; and although such trends would be in keeping with parental investment formulations under these two conditions, whether such differences are consistent must await more data on greater numbers of relatively young subjects in the two conditions, and perhaps observations of a species such as *M. nemestrina* in which normative levels of weaning are higher than those in the generally non-rejecting bonnets. At present however there is little clear evidence regarding the role that the mothers play in directly influencing the more independent behavior observed in the HFD infants.

In conclusion, we feel that the foregoing reflects the importance of considering the structure of primate groups within specific feeding ecologies and the potential impact of such structural variations upon the course of development of the infants within them. It is our hope that these preliminary data mark the opening of a series of new directions in the studies of primate development. It is clear moreover that, in this domain at least, the salient ingredients identified within field perspectives can be replicated within the controlled confines of the laboratory. This fact suggests a most significant opportunity to test a host of important hypotheses in the laboratory and to foster the meaningful exchange of material between field and laboratory that in the past has been more often honored in the breach than in the observance as an effective scientific synthesis.

ACKNOWLEDGMENTS

This research was supported in part by USPHS grant #MH 15965 and the State University of New York. The authors wish to thank Ms. Jayne Smiley for her considerable assistance in the conduct of this study.

REFERENCES

Altman, S. A. Baboons, space, time, and energy. *American Zoologist*, 1974, *14*, 221–248.
Ambrose, J. A. The ecological perspective in developmental psychology. In H. McGurk (Ed.), *Ecological factors in human development*. New York: North-Holland, 1977.

Anderson, C. O., Kenney, A. M. & Mason, W. A. Effects of maternal mobility, partner, and endocrine state on social responsiveness of adolescent rhesus monkeys. *Developmental Psychobiology, 10,* 1977, 421–434.

Azuma, S. Acquisition and propagation of food habits in a troop of Japanese monkeys. In C. R. Carpenter (Ed.), *Behavioral regulators of behavior in primates.* Cranbury, N.J.: Associated University Presses, 1973.

Baldwin, J. D., & Baldwin, J. I. Effects of food ecology on social play: A laboratory simulation. *Zeitschrift für Tierpsychology, 40,* 1976, 1–14.

Bekoff, M. Socialization in mammals with an emphasis on nonprimates. In S. Chevalier-Skolnikoff & F. E. Poirier (Eds.), *Primate bio-social development: biological, social, and ecological determinants.* New York: Garland, 1977.

Bernstein, I. C. Personal communication, 1970.

Bernstein, I. S. Activity profiles of primate groups. In *Behavior of nonhuman primates* (Vol. 3). New York: Academic Press, 1971.

Berry, J. Nomadic style and cognitive style. In H. McGurk (Ed.), *Ecological factors in human development.* New York: North-Holland, 1977.

Bronfenbrenner, U. Early deprivation in mammals and man. In G. Newton (Ed.), *Early experience and behavior.* Springfield, Ill.: C. C. Thomas, 1966.

Chalmers, N. R. Differences in behavior between some arboreal and terrestrial species of African monkeys. In R. R. Michael & J. H. Crook (Eds.), *Comparative ecology and behaviour of primates.* London: Academic Press, 1973.

Chalmers, N. R. Group composition, ecology and daily activities of free-living mangabeys in Uganda. *Folia Primatologica,* 1968, *8,* 247–262. (a)

Chalmers, N. R. The social behavior of free living mangabeys in Uganda. *Folia Primatologica,* 1968, *8,* 263–281. (b)

Chappell, P. F. Social behavior in interacting squirrel monkeys with differential nutritional and environmental histories. Paper presented at the Society for Research and Child Development. Denver, Colorado, 1977.

Charles-Dominique, P. *Ecology and behavior of nocturnal primates.* (Translated by R. D. Martin). New York: Columbia University Press, 1977.

Cheney, D. L. The acquisition of rank and the development of reciprocal alliances among free-ranging immature baboons. *Behavioral Ecology and Sociobiology, 2,* 303–318, 1977.

Cheney, D. L. Interactions of immature male and female baboons with adult females. *Animal Behaviour,* 1978, *26,* 389–408.

Chevalier-Skolnikoff, S., & Poirier, F. E. (Eds.) *Primate bio-social development: Biological, social, and ecological determinants.* New York: Garland, 1977.

Chivers, D. J. The feeding behavior of Siamang (*Symphalangus syndactyns*). In T. H. Clutton-Brock (Ed.), *Primate ecology: Studies of feeding and ranging behaviour in lemurs, monkeys and apes.* London: Academic Press, 1977.

Clutton-Brock, T.H. Some aspects of intraspecific variation in feeding and ranging behavior in primates. In T. H. Clutton-Brock (Ed.), *Primate ecology: Studies of feeding and ranging behaviour in lemurs, monkeys, and apes.* London: Academic Press, 1977.

Clutton-Brock, T. H. Feeding behavior of red colobus and black and white colobus in East Africa. *Folia Primatologica,* 1975, *23,* 165–207.

Clutton-Brock, T. H. (Ed.). *Primate ecology: Studies of feeding and ranging behaviour in lemurs, monkeys, and apes.* London: Academic Press, 1977.

Coelho, A. M., Jr., Bramblett, C. A., & Quick, L. R. Social organization and food resource availability in primates: A socio-bioenergetic analysis of diet and disease hypothesis. *American Journal of Physical Anthropology,* 1977, *46,* 235–264.

Collier, G. Ecological view of incentive and consummatory behavior. Paper presented at the American Psychological Association Convention. Rutgers, The State University, New Jersey, 1978.

Collier, G. H., & Rovee-Collier, C. K., A comparative analysis of optimal foraging behavior: Laboratory simulations. In A. C. Kamil & T. Sargent (Ed.), *Foraging behavior: Ecological, ethological, and psychological approaches*. New York: Garland Press, 1980.

Crook, J. H., & Gartlan, J. S. Evolution of primate societies. *Nature*, 1966, *210*, 1200–1204.

Davidge, C. Activity patterns of chacma baboons (*Papio ursenus*) at Cape Point. *Zoologica Africana*, 1978, *13*, 143–155.

deWaal, F. B. M. Exploitative and familiarity-dependent support strategies in a colony of semi-free living chimpanzees. *Behaviour*, 1978, *66*, 268–312.

Dittus, W. *The ecology and behavior of the toque monkey (Macaca sinica)* Doctoral dissertation, University of Maryland, 1974.

Dittus, W. P. J. The social regulation of population density and age–sex distribution in the toque monkey. *Behaviour*, 1977, *63*, 281–322.

Dolhinow, P. Commentary. Rajecki et al.: Infantile attachment theory. *The Behavioral & Brain Sciences*, 1978, *3*, 443–444.

Eisenberg, J. F., Muckenhirn, N. A., & Rudran, R. The relation between ecology and social structure in primates. *Science*, 1972, *176*, 863–874.

Fady, J. C. Les jeux sociaux: Le compagnon de jeux chez les jeunes. (Observations chez *Macaca itus*). *Folia Primatologica*, 1969, *11*, 134–143.

Fairbanks, L. A., & Bird, J. Ecological correlates of interindividual distance in the St. Kitts vervet (*Cercopithecus aethiops sabaeus*). *Primates*, 1978, *19*, 605–614.

Fedigan, L. M. Roles and activities of male geladas (*Theropithecus galada*). *Behaviour*, 1972, *41*, 82–90.

Fedigan, L. M., & Fedigan, L. The social development of a handicapped infant in a free-living troop of Japanese monkeys. In S. Chevalier-Skolnikoff & F. E. Poirier (Eds.), *Primate bio-social development: Biological, social, and ecological determinants*. New York: Garland, 1977.

Ferster, C. B., Hammer, C., & Randolph, J. An experimental space combining individual and social performances. *Journal of the Experimental Analysis of Behavior*, 1968, *11*, 209–220.

Fossey, D., & Harcourt, A. H. Feeding ecology of free-ranging mountain gorilla (*Gorilla gorilla beringei*) In T. H. Clutton-Brock (Ed.), *Primate ecology: Studies of feeding and ranging behaviour in lemurs, monkeys and apes*. London: Academic Press, 1977.

Freese, G. H. The behavior of white-faced capuchins (*Cebus capucinus*) at a dry-season waterhole. *Primates*, 1978, *19*, 275–286.

Frisch, J. E. Individual behavior and intertroop variability in Japanese macaques. In P. Jay (Ed.), *Primates: Studies in adaptation and variability*. New York: Holt, Rinehart and Winston, 1968.

Gard, G. C., & Meier, G. W. Social and contextual factors of play behavior in sub-adult rhesus monkeys. *Primates*, 1977, *18*, 367–377.

Gartlan, J. S. Adaptive aspects of social structure in *Erythrocebus patas*. In S. Kondo, M. Kawai, A. Ehara, & S. Kawamura (Eds.), *Proceedings from the Symposia of the Fifth Congress of the International Primatological Society*. Nagoyo, Japan, August 1974.

Gartlan, J. S., & Brain, C. K. Ecology and social variability in *Cercopithecus aethiops*. In P. Jay (Ed.), *Primates: Studies in adaptation and variability*. New York: Holt, Rinehart & Winston, 1968.

Gelles, R. J. Child abuse in psychopathology: A sociological critique and reformulation. In S. Chess & A. Thomas (Eds.), *Annual Progress in Child Psychiatry and Child Development*. New York: Brunner/Mazel, 1974.

Giovannoni, J. M., & Billingsly, A. Child neglect among the poor: A study of parental adequacy in families of three ethnic groups. In S. Chess & A. Thomas (Eds.), *Annual Progress in Child Psychiatry and Child Development*. New York: Brunner/Mazel, 1971.

Golden, M., & Birns, B. Social class and cognitive development in infancy. In S. Chess & A. Thomas (Eds.), *Annual Progress in Child Psychiatry and Child Development*. New York: Brunner/Mazel, 1969.

Hainsworth, F. F. & Wolf, L. L. Feeding: An ecological approach. In *Advances in the study of behavior* (Vol. 9). New York: Academic Press, 1979.

Hall. K. R. L. Behavior and ecology of the wild patas monkey *Erythrocebus patas,* in Uganda. In P. Jay (Ed.), *Primates: Studies in adaptation and variability.* New York: Holt, Rinehart & Winston, 1968.

Harlow, H. F. The nature of love. *American Psychologist,* 1958, *13,* 673–685.

Harlow, H. F. Age-mate or peer affectional system. *Advances in the Study of Behavior,* 1969, *2,* 333–383.

Herzog, E., & Lewis, H. Children in poor families. *Annual Progress in Child Psychiatry and Child Development.* New York: Brunner/Mazel, 1971.

Hinde, R. H. Development of social behavior. In *Behavior of nonhuman primates* (Vol. 3). New York: Academic Press, 1971.

Holmberg, A. R. Nomad of the long bow: The Siriono of Eastern Bolivia. Washington: Smithsonian Institute of Social Anthropology. Publication No. 10, U.S. Government Printing Office, 1950.

Horr, D. A. Orang-utan maturation: Growing up in a female world. In Chevalier-Skolnikoff & Poirier (Eds.), *Primate bio-social development: Biological, social, and ecological determinants.* New York: Garland, 1977.

Hrdy, S. B. *The langurs of Abu.* Cambridge, Mass.: Harvard University Press, 1977.

Itiogawa, N. Group organization of a natural troop of Japanese monkeys and mother–infant interactions. In C. R. Carpenter (Ed.), *Behavioral regulators of behavior in primates.* Cranbury, N.J.: Associated University Presses, 1973.

Izawa, K. A field study of the ecology and behavior of the black-mantle tamarin (*Saguinus nigricollis*). *Primates,* 1978, *19,* 241–274.

Jay, P. C. (Ed.) *Primates: Studies in adaptation and variability.* New York: Holt, Rinehart & Winston, 1968.

Jensen, G. D., Bobbitt, R. A., & Gordon, B. N. Patterns and sequences of hitting behavior in mothers and infant monkeys (*Macaca nemestrina*). *Journal of Psychiatric Research,* 1969, *7,* 55–61.

Jensen, G. D., Bobbitt, R. A., & Gordon, B. N. Effects of environment on the relationship between mothers and infant pigtailed monkeys (*Macaca nemestrina*). *Journal of Comparative and Physiological Psychology,* 1968, *66,* 259–263.

Kanarek, R. B. Energetics of meal patterns in rats. *Physiology and Behavior,* 1976, *17,* 395–399.

Kaplan, J. Differences in the mother–infant relations of squirrel monkeys housed in social and restricted environments. *Developmental Psychobiology,* 1972, *5,* 43–52.

Katz, I. A new approach to the study of school motivation in minority group children. In V. L. Allen (Ed.), *Psychological factors in poverty.* Chicago: Markham, 1970.

Kaufman, L. W., Collier, G., & Brashier, D. Optimal foraging in chickens. *American Naturalist* (in press).

Kawabe, M., & Mano, T. Ecology and behavior of the wild proboscis monkey. *Nasalis larvatus* (Wurmb), in Sabah, Malaysia. *Primates,* 1972, *13,* 213–228.

Kinzey, W. G. Diet and feeding behavior of *Callicebus torquatus.* In T. H. Clutton-Brock (Ed.), *Primate ecology: Studies of feeding and ranging behaviour in lemurs, monkeys and apes.* London: Academic Press, 1977.

Klein, L. L., & Klein, D. B. Feeding behavior of the Columbian spider monkey. In T. H. Clutton-Brock (Ed.), *Primate ecology: studies of feeding and ranging behaviour in lemurs, monkeys and apes.* London: Academic Press, 1977.

Koford, C. B. Ranks of mother and sons in bonds of rhesus monkeys. *Science,* 1963, *141,* 356–357.

Konner, M. Evolution of human behavior development. In P. H. Leiderman, S. R. Tulkin, and A. Rosenfeld (Eds.), *Culture and infancy: Variation in the human experience.* New York: Academic Press, 1977.

Kummer, H. *Social organization of hamadryas baboons: A field study.* Chicago: University of Chicago Press, 1968.

Kummer, H., & Kurt, F. A comparison of social behavior in captive and wild Hamadryas baboons. In H. Vogtborg (Ed.), *The baboon in medical research*. Austin: University of Texas Press, 1965.

Lamb, M. E., Suomi, S. J., & Stephenson, G. R. (Eds.) *Social interaction analysis*. Madison: University of Wisconsin Press, 1979.

Leiderman, P. H., & Leiderman, G. F. Economic change and infant care in an East African agricultural community. In Leiderman, Tulkin, & Rosenfeld (Eds.), *Culture and infancy: Variation in the human experience*. New York: Academic Press, 1977.

Leiderman, P. H., Tulkin, S. R., & Rosenfeld, A. (Eds.) *Culture and infancy: Variation in the human experience*. New York: Academic Press, 1977.

Levine, R. A. Child rearing as cultural adaptation. In P. H. Leiderman, S. R. Tulkin, and A. Rosenfeld (Eds.), *Culture and infancy: Variation in the human experience*. New York: Academic Press, 1977.

Lewis, M., & Freedle, R. The mother and infant communication system: The effects of poverty. In H. McGurk (Ed.), *Ecological factors in human development*. New York: North-Holland, 1977.

Lewis, M. & Goldberg, S. Perceptual-cognitive development in infancy: A generalized expectancy model as a function of mother-infant interaction. *Merrill-Palmer Quarterly*, 1969, *15*, 81-100.

Loy, J. Behavioral responses of free-ranging rhesus monkeys to food shortage. *American Journal of Physical Anthropology*, 1970, *33*, 272-363.

MacArthur, R. H., & Pianka, E. R. On the optimal use of a patchy environment. *American Natur.*, 1966, *100*, 603-609.

Marsden, H. H. Agonistic behavior of young rhesus monkeys after changes induced in social rank of their mothers. *Animal Behaviour*, 1968, *16*, 38-44.

Marsden, H. M. The effect of food deprivation on intergroup relations in rhesus monkeys. *Behavioral Biology*, 1972, *7*, 369-374.

Martin, B. Parent-child relations. In *Review of child development research* (Vol. 4). Chicago, University of Chicago Press, 1975.

Marwine, A. & Collier, G. The rat at the waterhole. *Journal of Comparative and Physiological Psychology*, 1979, *93*, 391-402.

Maslow, A. H. III. A theory of sexual behavior of infrahuman primates. *Journal of Genetic Psychology*, 1936, *48*, 310-338.

Mason, W. A., Social experience and primate cognitive development. In G. M. Burghardt & M. Bekoff (Eds.), *The development of behavior: Comparative and evolutionary aspects*. New York: Garland, 1978.

Mason, W. A., & Berkson, G. Effects of maternal mobility on the development of rocking and other behaviors in rhesus monkeys: A study with artificial mothers. *Developmental Psychobiology*, 1975, *8*, 213-221.

Mineka, S. & Suomi, S. Social separation in monkeys. *Psychological Bulletin*, 1978, *85*, 1376-1400.

Mitchell, G. D. Attachment differences in male and female infant monkeys. *Child Development*, 1968, *39*, 611-619.

Moore, R., & Young, D. Childhood outdoors: Toward a social ecology of landscape. In I. Altmann & J. F. Wohlwill (Eds.), *Human behavior and environment: Advances in theory and research* (Vol. 1). New York: Plenum, 1978.

Murphy, C. M., & Messer, D. J. Mothers, infants, and pointing: A study of gesture. In H. R. Schaffer (Ed.), *The origins of human social relations: Proceedings*. New York: Academic Press, 1971.

Murphy, D. E. Enrichment and occupational devices for orangutans and chimpanzees. *International Zoo News*, 137, July/Aug. 1976, 24-26.

Nash, L. T. The development of the mother-infant relationship in wild baboons (*Papio anubis*). *Animal Behaviour*, 1978, *26*, 746-759.

Natelson, B. H., & Bonbright, J. C. Jr. Patterns of eating and drinking in monkeys when food and water are free and when they are earned. *Physiology and Behavior,* 1978, *21,* 201–213.

Nicolson, N. A. A comparison of early behavioral development in wild and captive chimpanzees. In S. Chevalier-Skolnikoff & F. E. Poirier (Eds.), *Primate bio-social development: Biological, social, and ecological determinants.* New York, Garland, 1977.

Parthasarathy, M. D. Personal communication, 1979.

Pavenstadt, E. A comparison of the child-rearing environment of upper-lower and very lower-lower class families. *American Journal of Orthopsychiatry,* 196, *35,* 89–98.

Plotnik, R., King, F. A., & Rogers, L. Effects of competition on the aggressive behavior of squirrel and cebus monkeys. *Behaviour,* 1968, *32,* 315–332.

Poirier, F. E. The nilgiri langur (*Presbytis johnii*) troop: Its competition, structure, function and change. *Folia Primatologica,* 1969, *10,* 20–47.

Poirier, F. E. The nilgiri langur (*Presbytis johnii*) mother–infant dyad. *Primates,* 1968, *9,* 45–68.

Poirier, F. E. Introduction. In S. Chevalier-Skolnikoff & F. E. Poirier (Eds.), *Primate bio-social development: Biological, social, and ecological determinants.* New York, Garland, 1977.

Pyke, G. H., Pulliam, H. R., Charnov, E. L. Optimal foraging: A selective review of theory and tests. *The Quarterly Review of Biology,* 1977, *52,* 137–154.

Rahaman, H., & Parthasarathy, M. D. Studies on the social behavior of bonnet monkeys. *Primates,* 1969, *10,* 149–162.

Ransom, T. W., & Rowell, T. E. Early social development of feral baboons. In F. Poirier (Ed.), *Primate socialization.* New York: Random House, 1972.

Ricciuti, H. Adverse social biological influences on early development. In H. McGurk (Ed.), *Ecological factors in human development.* New York: North-Holland, 1977.

Rhine, R. J., & Westlund, B. J. The nature of primary feeding habit in different age–sex classes of yellow baboons (*Papio cynocephalus*). *Folia Primatologica,* 1978, *30,* 60–79.

Richard, A. Intra-specific variation in the social organization and ecology of *Propithecus verreauxi. Folia Primatologica,* 1974, *22,* 178–207.

Richard, A. The feeding behavior of *Propithecus verreauxi.* In T. H. Clutton-Brock (Ed.), *Primate ecology: Studies of feeding and ranging behaviour in lemurs, monkeys and apes.* London: Academic Press, 1977.

Rosenblum, L. A. Infant attachment in monkeys. In R. Schaffer (Ed.), *The origins of human social relations.* New York: Academic Press, 1971.

Rosenblum, L. A. Sex differences, environmental complexity, and mother–infant relations. *Archives of Sexual Behavior,* 1974, *11,* 117–128. (a)

Rosenblum, L. A. Sex differences in mother–infant relations in monkeys. In R. L. Vandewiele, R. M. Richart and R. C. Friedman (Eds.), *Sex differences in behavior.* New York: Wiley, 1974. (b)

Rosenblum, L. A. Affective maturation and the mother-infant relationship. In M. Lewis and L. A. Rosenblum (Eds.), *The development of affect.* New York: Plenum Press, 1978.

Rosenblum, L. A. Monkeys in time and space: A situational taxonomy for the study of nonhuman primates in the laboratory. In M. Lamb, S. J. Suomi, & G. Stephenson (Eds.), *Social interaction analysis: Methodological issues.* Madison: University of Wisconsin Press, 1979.

Rosenblum, L. A., & Alpert, S. Response to mother and stranger: A first step in socialization. *In* Chevalier-Skolnikoff, S. and Poirier, F. E. (Eds.). *Primate bio-social development: Biological, social, and ecological determinants.* New York: Garland Publishing, 1977, pp. 463–478.

Rosenblum, L. A., Coe, C., & Bromley, L. Peer relations in monkeys: The influence of social structure, gender and familiarity. In M. Lewis & L. A. Rosenblum (Eds.), *The origins of behavior: Peer relations and friendships.* New York: Wiley, 1975.

Rosenblum, L. A., & Kaufman, I. C. Laboratory observations of early mother–infant relations in pigtail and bonnet macaques. In: S. A. Altmann (Ed.), *Social communication among primates,* Chicago: University of Chicago Press, 1967.

Rosenblum, L. A., Kaufman, I. C., & Stynes, A. J. Interspecific variations in the effects of hunger of diurnally varying behavior elements in macaques. *Brain, Behavior, and Evolution,* 1969, *2,* 119-131.

Rosenblum, L. A., & Smiley, J. Developmental weight gain in two species of macaque and the onset of progression of obesity in bonnet macaques. *Journal of Medical Primatology,* 1980, *9,* 247-253.

Rosenblum, L. A. & Plimpton, E. H. The effects of adults on peer interaction. In M. Lewis & L. A. Rosenblum (Eds.), *The child and its family.* New York: Plenum Press, 1979.

Rowell, T. E. A quantitative comparison of the behavior of a wild and a caged baboon group. *Animal Behavior,* 1967, *15,* 499-509.

Rowell, T. E. The concept of social dominance. *Behavioral Biology,* 1974, *11,* 131-154.

Rowell, T. E., Din, N. A., & Omar, A. The social development of baboons in their first three months. *Journal of Zoology,* 1968, *155,* 461-483.

Sackett, G. P., Holm, R. A., Rupenthal, G. C., & Farhrenbruch, C. E. The effects of total social isolation rearing on behavior of rhesus and pigtail macaques. In R. N. Walsh & W. T. Greenough (Eds.), *Environments as therapy for brain dysfunction.* New York: Plenum, 1976.

Sade, D. S. *Am. J. phys. Anthrop.* 1965, *23,* 1-23.

Sameroff, A. J. Early influences on development; fact or fancy? In S. Chess & A. Thomas (Eds.), *Annual progress in child psychiatry and child development.* New York: Brunner/Mazel, 1976.

Schoener, T. W. Theory of feeding strategies. *Annual Review Ecology & Systematics,* 1971, *2,* 379-404.

Seyfarth, R. M. A model of social grooming among adult female monkeys. *Journal of Theoretical Biology,* 1977, *65,* 671-698.

Slocum, J., & Strobel, D. Mother-infant behavior in protein deficient rhesus macaques. Paper presented at the 45th annual meeting of the American Association of Physical Anthropologists, St. Louis, April 1976.

Southwick, C. H. An experimental study of intragroup agonistic behavior in rhesus monkeys (*Macaca mulatta*). *Behaviour,* 1967, *28,* 182-209.

Southwick, C. H., Siddiqi, M. F., Farooqui, M. Y., & Pal, B. C. Effects of artificial feeding on aggressive behavior of rhesus monkeys in India. *Animal Behaviour,* 1976, *24,* 11-15.

Spuhler, J. N., & Jorche, L. B. Primate phylogeny, ecology, and social behavior. *Journal of Anthropological Research,* 1975, *31,* 376-405.

Stevenson, M. Observations of maternal behavior and infant development in the deBrazza monkey. (*Cercopithecus neglectus*) in captivity. *International Zoo Yearbook, 13,* 1973, 179-184.

Struhsaker, T. T., & Leland, L. Socioecology of five sympatric monkey species in the Kibale Forest, Uganda. In J. S. Rosenblatt, R. A. Hinde, C. Beer, & M. Busnel (Eds.), *Advances in the study of behavior.* New York: Academic Press, 1979.

Sussman, R. W. Socialization, social structure, and ecology of two sympatric species of lemur. In S. Chevalier-Skolnikoff & F. E. Poirier (Eds.), *Primate bio-social development: Biological, social, and ecological determinants.* New York: Garland, 1977.

Trivers, R. L. Parent-offspring conflict. *American Zoologist,* 1974, *14,* 249-264.

Wallston, B. The effects of maternal employment on children. In S. Chess & A. Thomas (Eds.), *Annual progress in child psychiatry and child development.* New York: Brunner/Mazel, 1971.

Warren, J. M., & Maroney, R. J. Competitive social interaction between monkeys. *Journal of Social Psychology,* 1958, *48,* 23-233.

Wilson, E. O. *Sociobiology: The new synthesis,* Cambridge, Mass.: Harvard University Press, 1975.

Wolfheim, J. H., Jensen, G. D., & Bobbitt, R. A. Effects of group environment on the mother-infant relationship in pigtailed monkeys (*Macaca nemestrina*). *Primates,* 1970, *11,* 119-124.

Wrangham, R. W. Artificial feeding of chimpanzees and baboons in their natural habitat. *Animal Behaviour,* 1974, *22,* 83-93.

Wu, H. M. H., & Holmes, W. G. Kin preference in infant *Macaca nemestrina*. In G. W. Barlow & J. Silbergerg (Eds.), *Sociobiology: Beyond nature–nurture*. Washington, D.C.: AAAS Publication, in press.

Zimmerman, R. R., Geist, C. R., & Ackles, P. R. Changes in the social behavior of rhesus monkeys during rehabilitation from prolonged protein-caloric malnutrition. *Behavioral Biology*, 1975, *14*, 325–333.

5 Parenting, Prosocial Behavior, and Political Attitudes

Paul Mussen
University of California, Berkeley

This chapter deals with the consequences of parenting, particularly with the consequences of several parental practices on the development of children's prosocial behavior. The term *prosocial behavior* refers to actions that are intended to aid or benefit others without the actor's anticipation of external rewards. Included are acts of generosity, altruism, and sympathy; helping people in distress by giving material or psychological assistance; sharing possessions; donating to charity; and participating in activities dedicated to reduction of social injustices and improvement of the general welfare. Prosocial actions often entail self-sacrifice, cost, or risk for the actor. The history of psychological study of these behaviors is a brief one, essentially covering only the last 20 or 25 years. The bulk of the relevant research has been conducted by students of socialization who, like me, sought to discover the psychological processes underlying the acquisition of prosocial behavior: training, learning, imitation, and cognitive factors such as insight and understanding. We paid little attention to biological variables, for the actions that interested us did not appear, at least on the surface, to have any direct links with genes, hormones, or nervous system functions.

The focus of this chapter is the development of altruism and consideration of others. Because in recent years sociobiologists have focused much attention on the possible biological bases of altruistic behavior and so much of this volume is biologically oriented, it behooves me to say a few words about these matters. I take issue with the sociobiologists' assumption that for human beings, as for other species, altruism has adaptive or inclusive fitness value and is the product of evolutionary forces; there is no convincing evidence that human proclivities for altruism are genetically determined. In a recent chapter in *Sociobiology and Human Nature*, Frank Beach (1978) criticized—properly in my opinion—the

111

sociobiologists' tendency to compare presumably similar behavior of different species without fully analyzing the motivations and mediational components of these behaviors. He specifically attacked the notion that there is a unitary type of behavior occurring in different species and justifying the common label of homosexuality. An analogous criticism applies of course to the concept of altruism. The honey bee workers' suicidal self-sacrifice in killing intruders threatening the hive—thus saving their fellow honey bees—and the mother partridge's feigning of injury—thus risking her life to distract a predator's attention from her young—are undoubtedly built-in, genetically determined responses. But they can hardly be considered in the same category as instances of human altruism that occur in the context of interpersonal relations and involve conscious intent and cognitive mediating processes. As Gunther Stent (1977) pointed out in a review of Dawkins' book, *The Selfish Gene,* such sociobiological playing with the word *altruism* is unlikely to contribute much to our understanding of moral or prosocial behavior.

Certainly attempts to discover the biological foundations of social behavior, including prosocial behavior, must be encouraged. Psychologists have not traditionally been good at this, and they have often prematurely dismissed possible biological correlates of social responses. It now seems clear that there is no polarity between biology and socialization practices; the two are intimately interrelated. As Washburn (1976) has pointed out: "It is biology that learns and to emphasize learning in no way removes biological considerations . . . [p. 354]." We can only respond to socialization training through the mechanisms of our body; we learn and think through the cortex; and we cannot feel without the limbic and endocrine systems. There is little doubt, however, that social responses vary in the extent to which they involve genetic factors, and experience suggests that most social responses can be modified through socialization.

At the same time, it seems quite likely that biological factors set the limit of the reaction range, facilitating or restricting the individual's capacities to react in certain ways. For example, from the earliest hours of life, some babies cry easily and are hard to console (Caucasians), but others cry less and can be soothed readily (Chinese) (Freedman & Freedman, 1969). The early appearance of these individual differences and the fact that they are characteristic of different populations suggests a constitutional basis for these temperamental characteristics. It seems reasonable to postulate that these differences are related to proneness to empathy which is probably one of the most basic components of altruism. But the forms and qualities of altruism, as well as the situations in which altruism is likely to be expressed, are shaped primarily by socialization practices. As Sherwood Washburn (1976) has pointed out "the more learning is basic, the less will there be any simple relationship between genes and behaviors [p. 354]."

Regardless of what we believe to be the connections between biological factors and social behavior, we must recognize that biological research on these matters is very difficult and time consuming; results that have clear implications for social action are not likely to be achieved in the near future. Meanwhile we are almost daily bombarded with impressive evidence of our society's critical needs for improved social interactions—for more kindness, consideration, generosity, and altruism. Clearly we cannot wait for the results of research on the biological determinants of prosocial behavior before doing something about the situation. Having demonstrated that parental socialization practices have significant impacts on such negative social characteristics as aggression, overdependency, delinquency, and maladjustment, researchers in socialization must pursue with all deliberate speed and with vigor their attempts to understand how parenting can help foster and amplify prosocial responses. Their work does not have to await findings of biological research. Fortunately the last 15 years have witnessed a significant, if not auspicious, beginning of research on the development of prosocial behavior. Let us now turn our attention to some highly relevant facts that have been established.

In theory any or all parenting procedures—that is, child-rearing practices and disciplinary techniques—can influence children's prosocial behavior: demonstration or modeling (performing behaviors that the child can emulate); material rewards; nurturance (caring for the child with warmth, support, and affection); praise and approval; giving or withholding love; explanation and example of rules; lecturing and giving "lessons"; corporal and psychological punishment. Not all of these parenting practices have been investigated systematically, but several of them have been. In reviewing studies, I stress those from which we can draw conclusions about the kinds of parenting that foster or hinder the development of prosocial behavior. The studies of greatest merit, in my opinion, are those that have ecological validity, that is, studies that are to a large extent naturalistic, assessing independent (parental) and dependent (prosocial) variables of substantial duration or stability as they are manifested in the real world. Experiments in highly contrived situations, using limited or artificial measures of either parenting or consequent prosocial behavior, are not likely to tell us much about how real children in the real world respond to their parents' actual behavior.

Given these constraints, we can discern at least three aspects of parenting that are of proven power in shaping children's prosocial behavior. These will be presented in order of the weight of the evidence about their influence; that is, where the evidence of the impacts of modeling and imitation is most compelling: So studies of these parental practices will be reviewed first. Of course that doesn't mean that modeling is actually the most potent influence—although, as you will see, I believe it is—or that the second practice, induction or reasoning in discipline, affects the child's tendencies to behave in prosocial ways more strongly than parental maintenance of high standards, the third aspect of parenting to be discussed. And it is entirely possible that certain other aspects of parenting, whose consequences for prosocial behavior have not been systematically studied—for example, consistency of discipline, promotion of self-esteem, family discussions of moral issues—have even more profound effects. These are as yet unsolved questions, questions that must become the foci of systematic research in the future.

MODELING AND IDENTIFICATION

Children who observe a model performing some prosocial act (donating to a charity, helping another, or sharing goodies) are likely to emulate these acts immediately and often a long time afterward. This finding has been replicated in many experimental studies. Analogously, modeling of prosocial behavior by parents, especially by nurturant parents, apparently has enduring positive effects on the development of altruism and helping behavior as a number of studies attest.

Once in a while ingenious investigators duplicate real-life home situations realistically in an experimental setting and study the effects of different treatments on children's prosocial responses. For example, in one excellent recent experiment on the effects of modeling, the model was well known to the nursery school children who participated in the study. She took care of them 5 days a week for 2 weeks and established meaningful relationships with them. In addition, she modeled altruistic behavior several times in two sessions separated by 2 days (Yarrow, Scott, & Waxler, 1973).

Before beginning their experiment the investigators assessed the children's original propensities for helping by observing their reactions to pictures of people or animals in distress—for example, a child with a bleeding knee falling off a bike—and to four actual behavioral instances of distress, such as a kitten tangled in yarn struggling toward its mother.

In the experiment itself the children observed the caretaker–model acting in helpful ways in different situations. Some children were exposed only to "symbolic altruism," modeled in dioramas (miniature reproductions) of scenes of distress involving children, families, or animals. There were duplicates of each diorama set; the model had one and the child had the other. As described by Yarrow et al (1973) the adult's modeling always included:

> (a) verbalized awareness of the distress, (b) her sympathy and help for the victim, (c) her pleasure or relief at the comfort or well-being that resulted, and (d) her use of the word "help" to summarize what had been done. For example, she turned to the first diorama, a monkey trying to reach the banana, and said, "Oh, Mr. Monkey, you must be hungry. You can't reach your food. I'll help you. Here's your banana. Now you won't be hungry." She then uncovered the paired diorama and told the child that it was his or her turn. If the child retrieved the banana for the monkey, the adult said, "I think the monkey feels better because you gave him his food. He isn't hungry now." If the child did not help, the adult went on to the next set of dioramas, repeating the procedures [p. 246].

Another group of children observed another kind of modeling; they too were exposed to "symbolic altruism" (with dioramas) and in addition the adult actually modeled altruism to another individual. For example, at one point during training another adult came into the room, tried to retrieve something under the table, and banged her head. She winced and held her head. The model responded warmly, putting her hand on the confederate's shoulder and saying, "I hope you aren't hurt. Do you want to sit down a minute?" The victim responded appreciatively.

With half the children, in each modeling condition the model was nurturant, initiating friendly interactions, offering help and support freely, sympathizing and protecting, and praising them frequently. With the other half of the children, the model was nonnurturant; she was aloof, gave only minimum help, and generally disregarded the children's achievements or was critical of them.

Two days after the last training session, the altruistic responses of the children were assessed again, using a new series of pictures and dioramas plus two actual behavioral incidents involving distress. Then, 2 weeks after that, there was an additional testing session outside the nursery school, to measure the durability and generalization of the effects of modeling. In this session the children were taken individually to a neighboring house to visit a mother and her baby and while there could help the mother by picking up a basket of spools or buttons that had spilled or by retrieving toys the baby had dropped out of her crib.

The two types of modeling had vastly different consequences. Modeling "symbolic altruism," that is, modeling with dioramas only, produced less increment in altruistic responses than training involving "symbolic altruism" *and* modeling of helping in actual "live" interactions. On the tests given 2 days after the end of the training, those trained exclusively with dioramas showed increased altruism *only* in diorama situations; their altruism did not extend or generalize to pictured situations or to behavioral incidents. The differential effects of the two kinds of modeling were most apparent on the follow-up test 2 weeks later. Those who had observed extended modeling, including aid to another individual, by a nurturant adult were more likely to express sympathy and to help the mother or baby in the home setting, than children in any other group. Eighty-four percent of these children spontaneously gave help in this situation, although only 24% of them had helped in the original, pretraining behavioral incidents.

Extrapolating from these results, the investigators (Yarrow et al., 1973) have these suggestions about parenting and prosocial behavior:

The parent who conveys his values to the child didactically as tidy principles, and no more, accomplishes only that learning in the child. Generalized altruism would appear to be best learned from parents who do not only try to inculcate the principles of altruism, but who also manifest altruism in everyday interactions. . . . Evidence on the role of nurturance in the rearing environment does not suggest that it is sufficient. The data demonstrate its importance along with the specific modelling accompanied by the model's verbal communications [p. 256].

More clinical, correlational studies confirm and extend the findings of this experimental study, demonstrating that repeated adult modeling, particularly by a nurturant model, produces powerful, generalized effects. In one study the generosity of nursery school boys was measured in terms of the amount of candy (won in a game) they were willing to share with friends. (This measure was significantly correlated with independent ratings of generosity by the nursery school teachers.) The most generous and the least generous subsequently completed some incomplete doll play stories and in doing this expressed their perceptions of their parents, of themselves, and of their interactions with their parents. Compared with the stingy boys the generous ones much more frequently portrayed their fathers as models of generosity, sympathy, and compassion and as nurturant and warm parents. These characteristics foster strong identification with the parent, and consequently imitation of that parent's patterns of generosity and sympathy (Rutherford & Mussen, 1968).

A number of fascinating clinical investigations of the development of unusually altruistic adults reinforce these findings on early parental modeling as a prime antecedent of consistent and stable altruism. One was a study of 27 Christians who risked their lives during World War II by rescuing Jews from the Nazis. Among the most outstanding, prevalent characteristics of these individuals was intense identification with a parent who was a significant model of moral orientation and conduct. Some of these parents were religious moralists and others were moral idealists; in all cases they were models with whom the altruists identified (London, 1970).

Another clinical study, conducted by Rosenhan, involved Freedom Riders, civil rights movement workers in the '50s and '60s—people who marched in parades, protested, picketed, and gave speeches on behalf of improved status for blacks (Rosenhan, 1969). Among them was a group that could be labeled *fully committed,* workers who were active in the movement for a long period of time, often giving up their homes, occupations, and education to engage in civil rights work at the risk of being insulted, humiliated, beaten, or even murdered. Extensive and intensive interviews with these workers indicated that parental identification and nurturance were critically important antecedents of their altruistic behavior. When they were children, their parents had worked vigorously in behalf of altruistic causes, protesting against Nazi atrocities, religious restrictions, or other injustices. The Freedom Riders had witnessed their parents' commitment and efforts; they also shared their parents' emotions. In addition they viewed their parents as warm, respecting, and loving during their childhood and early adulthood.

The findings of all these developmental studies may be summarized succinctly. Observation of strong and consistent models, such as parents and other caretakers, who manifest their own prosocial dispositions in words and deeds is highly conducive to the development of strong, enduring tendencies toward prosocial behavior in children. The modeling and identification effects are particularly strong if in addition to demonstrating prosocial behavior caretakers behave in nurturant and loving ways toward their children.

USE OF INDUCTION IN DISCIPLINE

In addition to serving as models, parents or caretakers have to discipline their children, and the specific disciplinary techniques they use may have effects on the development of their children's tendencies toward prosocial behavior. Use of physical force or threat by parents may be perceived by the child as evidence that aggression may be an effective way of achieving some goals, but it probably makes the child hostile. If parents reason with their children, pointing out the "rights" and "wrongs" of their actions, they inevitably model consideration for others, and at the same time they clarify the implications of the children's behavior for others and stress empathy as an important component of social interactions.

The most relevant research on these issues was designed and conducted by Professor Martin Hoffman and his colleagues (Hoffman, 1975; Hoffman & Saltzstein, 1967). In one of their early studies they were concerned with consideration of others—which is one definition of altruism—and the participants were children in the seventh grade. The level of consideration was operationally defined by the number of peer nominations for the positions of the classmate "most likely to care about other children's feelings" and "most likely to defend a child being made fun of by the group." Disciplinary techniques were assessed in this way: Parents were asked to imagine four situations, for example, the child delaying complying with the parental request to do something, the child being careless and destroying something of value that belonged to another child. Then, using a list of possible reactions, they designated their three most likely reactions to each of these situations, for example, spanking the child, explaining how the other child would feel about the destruction of a toy. Some of the disciplinary practices were based on *power assertion,* that is, control by physical means or manipulation of material resources exemplified by physical force, deprivation of material objects or privileges, or the threat of these. Other practices involve *induction,* that is, the parent reasons with the child, explaining the painful consequences of the child's act for himself, for others, or for the parent—for example, telling the child how his or her actions hurt the parent or making reference to concern for another child.

Frequent use of power assertion by the mother was associated with *low* levels of consideration for others whereas repeated use of induction was positively correlated with this type of prosocial behavior. In short a pattern of infrequent use of power assertion and liberal use of induction by mothers facilitates the development of prosocial behavior—at least in the middle class. This is largely attributable, the investigators believe, to the fact that induction is "most capable of eliciting the child's natural proclivities for empathy [Hoffman & Saltzstein, 1967, p. 558]." Power assertive techniques, on the other hand, are least effective in stimulating the development of consideration for others because in using this technique, the parent communicates that the appropriate bases for deciding on what action to take is external power and authority—such as the parent's—rather than appraisal of the consequences of one's actions for others.

Confirmation and extension of these findings on the effectiveness of induction are found in studies that employed different criteria of prosocial behavior and participants of different ages. For example, frequent use of induction by mothers, accompanied by low frequency of power assertion, has been found to be a significant antecedent of high levels of sensitivity to others' needs and of direct helpfulness to peers among preschool children.

In another study fifth and eighth grade students at a Catholic school answered questionnaires about their mothers' disciplinary techniques and nominated the classmates who were kindest and most considerate (Dlugokinski & Firestone, 1974). They were also given opportunities to donate money to UNICEF, a charitable organization, and they completed self-report forms on values, ranking in order of personal importance 12 statements such as "having a beautiful home and car" and "getting a job that helps other people." These rankings provided measures of each child's standing on self-centered values (material possessions, self-importance) or other-centered values (concern for others).

Mothers' use of inductive techniques was a good predictor of children's prosocial tendencies. At each age level studied sons and daughters of mothers who used induction in discipline were perceived as more considerate, attached more importance to other-centered than to self-centered values, and donated more to charity. In contrast use of power assertion by the mother was associated with self-centered values and stinginess in donations (Dlugokinski & Firestone, 1974).

The findings from these varied studies consistently lead to the same conclusion: Frequent use of induction techniques by parents promotes the development of prosocial tendencies whereas extensive use of power assertive techniques tends to diminish the level of children's prosocial behavior. There is no research evidence that indicates that sparing the rod will spoil the child.

MATURITY DEMANDS AND ASSIGNMENT OF RESPONSIBILITY

The last statement should not be taken to mean that what traditionally has been called permissive or laissez faire parenting is conducive to the development of high levels of prosocial behavior. On the contrary, recent in-depth studies of parenting by Diana Baumrind of the Institute of Human Development of the University of California suggest that parental control and high maturity demands are prime antecedents of high levels of prosocial behavior in children. Maturity demands include parents' high standards for the child as well as control and pressure on him or her to behave in mature ways, that is, to perform and achieve, and to assume responsibilities consistent with his or her level of maturity.

Such parental demands were associated with advanced levels of social responsibility among nursery school boys and girls, that is, with frequent altruistic and nurturant acts toward others, those being assessed independently by means of intensive, objective naturalistic observations by trained observers (Baumrind, 1971). Incidentally, in a longitudinal follow-up of these same children, Baumrind found remarkable consistency in manifestations of this characteristic over time: Children rated high in social responsibility during the preschool years continued to be highly socially responsible 5 or 6 years later, when they were observed in the third grade.

The assumption of responsibility is an integral part of maturity demands that enhance the prosocial behavior of children. This finding is entirely congruent with the cross-cultural findings of Whiting and Whiting (1975). Their data showed that children reared in cultures in which there is early assignment of responsibility manifest more altruistic, helping, and supportive behavior than children reared in cultures that do not follow this practice. Interestingly, in the Soviet Union, part of the elementary school curriculum consists of assuming responsibility for younger children. The purpose of assigning school responsibility is the enhancement of predispositions toward helping and sharing among the pupils. The data from the studies just reviewed here suggest that this goal can be achieved by this means.

Some data from my recent research in political socialization are also consistent with these findings about the role of the assignment of responsibility in the promotion of children's prosocial orientations (Eisenberg-Berg & Mussen, 1980). My assumption, frankly linked with my own value system, is that liberal sociopolitical attitudes are manifestations of underlying prosocial orientations. Because we wanted to explore parenting practices and personality correlates of the development of liberalism, it seemed sensible to try to study children in the early stages of political-attitude formation. Consequently our population consisted of over 200 junior and senior high school students who responded to a 41-item questionnaire that consisted of agree/disagree statements about a variety of current political issues, such as civil liberties, domestic welfare, and equality of opportunity. The 37 students scoring highest and the 35 scoring lowest in liberalism were then interviewed, tested and given Q sorts for personality self-evaluations and interactions with parents.

The liberal adolescents regarded themselves as more rebellious, independent in thinking, introspective, sympathetic, loving, and tender, but the conservatives perceived themselves as more conventional, responsible, dependable, orderly, neat, organized, successful, and ambitious. Most pertinent for our discussion here is the fact that the liberal children reported that their parents' child-rearing techniques emphasized the development of independence, personal responsibility, and emotional control whereas the parents of the conservatives stressed conventional and approved behavior, conformity with authority, and making good impressions on others. Again it appears that high standards and assumption of personal responsibility loom large in the development of liberal attitudes in children as they did in the development of altruism and nurturance of others.

It should be added however that our data make it clear that the development of liberalism among adolescents is very complex. For example, the conservative children reported that they had good relationships with their parents, whom they perceived as understanding, helpful, and affectionate, but the liberal boys and girls reported considerably more conflict with their parents. Some of these last findings are undoubtedly related to the fact that the study was conducted in a conservative, upper middle-class WASP community. The results pertaining to conflict with parents might be different if the participants came from different sociopolitical milieux (Eisenberg-Berg & Mussen, 1980).

To summarize, we can distill a number of substantial conclusions about the effects of variations in parenting on children's prosocial behavior from the data of these studies. These conclusions are not surprising or sensational. In fact, it appears that the techniques many sensible parents have used for millenia facilitate the development of prosocial behavior: identification and modeling prosocial behavior, especially if accompanied by nurturance; induction—that is, reasoning and explanation—rather than power assertion in disciplining the child; making reasonable demands for mature behavior. It is comforting to find scientific findings that support what is advocated in "folk wisdom."

A note of caution seems appropriate in closing. We are very far from a complete understanding of the problem of the influences of parenting and cognitive factors on the development of prosocial behavior. We still have more questions than answers. Consequences of many potentially powerful parenting techniques, such as democratic discussion of family problems or strict puritanical rearing, have not yet been systematically investigated, nor have the consequences of interactions among various types of determinants been researched. For example, what happens to the children whose parents are models of consideration and kindness if they live in a culture that stresses competition and selfishness? What we urgently need are more thorough naturalistic studies that preserve the inherent complexity of the determinants and reveal how interrelated factors operate in advancing or inhibiting the development of prosocial behavior.

REFERENCES

Baumrind, D. Current patterns of parental authority. *Developmental Psychology Monographs,* 1971, *1*, 1–103.

Beach, F. A. Sociobiology and interspecific comparisons of behavior. In M. S. Gregory, A. Silvers, & D. Sutch (Eds.), *Sociobiology and Human Nature.* San Francisco: Jossey-Bass, 1978.

Dlugokinski, E., & Firestone, I. J. Other-centeredness and susceptibility to charitable appeals: Effects of perceived discipline. *Developmental Psychology,* 1974, *10,* 21–28.

Eisenberg-Berg, N., & Mussen, P. Personality correlates of sociopolitical liberalism and conservatism in adolescents. *Journal of Genetic Psychology,* 1980, *137,* 165–177.

Freedman, D. G., & Freedman, N. C. Behavioral differences between Chinese-American and European-American newborns. *Nature,* 1969, *224* (5225), 1227.

Hoffman, M. L. Altruistic behavior and the parent–child relationship. *Journal of Personality and Social Psychology,* 1975, *31,* 937–943.

Hoffman, M. L., & Saltzstein, H. D. Parent discipline and the child's moral development. *Journal of Personality and Social Psychology,* 1967, *5,* 45–57.

London, P. The rescuers: Motivational hypotheses about Christians who saved Jews from the Nazis. In J. Macaulay & L. Berkowitz (Eds.), *Altruism and helping behavior.* New York: Academic Press, 1970.

Rosenhan, D. Some origins of concern for others. In P. Mussen, J. Langer, & M. Covington (Eds.), *Trends and issues in developmental psychology.* New York: Holt, Rinehart & Winston, 1969.

Rutherford, E., & Mussen, P. Generosity in nursery school boys. *Child Development,* 1968, *39,* 755–765.

Stent, G. S. You can take the ethics out of altruism but you can't take the altruism out of ethics. *The Hastings Center Report,* 1977, *7* (6), 33–36.

Washburn, S. L. Biological versus social evolution. *American Psychologist,* 1976, *31,* 353–355.

Whiting, B. B., & Whiting, J. W. M. *Children of six cultures: A psychocultural analysis.* Cambridge, Mass.: Harvard University Press, 1975.

Yarrow, M. R., Scott, P., & Waxler, C. Z. Learning concern for others. *Developmental Psychology,* 1973, *8,* 240–260.

6

Infant Distress: Variables Affecting Responses of Caregivers and Others

Alan R. Wiesenfeld
Carol Zander Malatesta
Douglass College
Rutgers University

INTRODUCTION

A great deal of modern research on infant socialization has been guided by the work of ethologically oriented workers such as Bowlby (1969) and Ainsworth (1969, 1972), who have emphasized the importance of caregiver responsiveness or sensitivity to infant cues in the development of the attachment relationship. Ainsworth (1972) has defined attachment as "an affectional tie or bond that one individual . . . forms between himself and another specific individual [p. 100]" and suggests that qualitative differences in infant–mother attachments may have as their precursors differences in the way mothers respond to the signals of the infant early in life. Ainsworth and her colleagues have developed several measures to index maternal sensitivity—for example, latency of response to infant cries, maternal behaviors during feeding such as bodily contact, *en face* orienting, pacing of feeding, and other subtle interactional phenomena (Ainsworth, 1969; Ainsworth, 1972; Bell & Ainsworth, 1972). Other developmentalists have also attempted to measure sensitivity. Field (1977) has recorded amount of maternal stimulation of the infant during "nipple in" and "nipple out" epochs in the feeding situation; Donovan and Leavitt (1978) have relied upon the timing of maternal stimulation during infant gaze-directed and gaze-averted periods.

Interest in developing sensitivity measures presumably derives from the assumption that caregivers who are receptive and responsive to infant signals provide a more optimal environment for the developing infant and that these caregiving qualities can be objectively measured. The development of reliable and valid sensitivity instruments may ultimately enable psychologists to predict the outcome of caregiver–infant relationships and to recommend appropriate

123

early interventions when there is indication that a particular relationship is drifting away from an optimal course.

One inherent problem with behavioral measures such as the aforementioned is that maternal behaviors occurring during limited observational periods may be susceptible to subtle demands to conform to socially desirable responses. As such, adjunctive measures of responsivity may be helpful in evaluating the validity of behavioral measures and in refining the concept of sensitivity. One such method involves direct physiological monitoring of caregivers' autonomic nervous system arousal during stimulation by infant signals. Within our own laboratory we are currently developing and exploring such measures. In the present chapter we describe our research on caregiver response to infant distress cries as well as some variables that may underlie "caregiver sensitivity," and which may be important considerations in evaluating the course of the developing infant–caregiver bond.

BACKGROUND

Crying is clearly the most fundamental and prepotent response in the young infant's behavioral repertoire. Human infants like the young of most other mammalian species, possess a built-in calling system, evoked in states of distress, that functions to alert parents or other adults. In some primate species only the mother responds to the signal; in others, both parents; and in some species the attention of other adults may be elicited (Epple, 1968, 1975; Klopfer, 1970; Redican, 1975; Takeda, 1965; van Lawick-Goodall, 1968, 1971). The infant distress-signalling system is unlearned, elicitable within a short time after birth, and ubiquitous across the diversity of mammalian species; it is clearly biologically adaptive. It seems reasonable to expect that reciprocal mechanisms of response exist in those adult members of the species in the position to provide protection and assistance.

The human cry is widely recognized as preemptory or compelling in character. We believe that the compelling nature of a cry resides partly in the stimulus itself and partly in the receptive capacities and qualities of the caregiver. Qualities of the cry that make it particularly hard to ignore include its high pitch and intensity; Ostwald (1972) maintains that the infant cry is one of the loudest sounds humans ever make and has likened it to the intensity of the noise of an unmuffled truck. The specific qualities of the listener are less well understood. Human mothers are described as being particularly responsive to infant cries. It is not yet certain however whether this responsiveness is a function of physiological priming due to the hormones of pregnancy and lactation, whether it is strictly a matter of learning or socialization and hence can be unlearned or turned off through adverse experience, or whether it is the product of both sets of influences (Murray, 1979). Research with animals indicates that both factors may be important (Amenomori, Chen, & Meites, 1970; Kuhn, 1969; Moltz, Lubin, Leon, & Numan, 1970; Rosenblatt, 1967, 1975; Siegel & Rosenblatt, 1975; Zarrow, Gandelman, & Denenberg, 1971).

Early research on sensitivity to human infant cries centered on the issue of whether there were detectable differences among the sounds of cries elicited under different circumstances and whether subjects were able to discriminate among cry types. In one of the first published studies of its kind Mandel Sherman (1927a, 1927b) presented observers with live and filmed presentations of crying neonates. The crying was elicited under conditions of hunger, sudden dropping, restraint of head and face, or pin prick. A wide variety of emotions were named in response to individual stimulus classes, and Sherman concluded that subjects were generally *unable* to associate the elicited cries with the stimulus situation without the benefit of contextual cues. In a similar study Aldrich, Sung, and Knopp (1945) asked subjects to identify the cause of crying in 1–8-day-old infants; these researchers were unable to obtain clear-cut response data because the majority of cases of crying were attributed by the subjects to "unknown causes." Using a wider age-range of infants (birth to 8 months) and prerecorded cries, Wasz-Hockert and co-workers (Wasz-Hockert, Partanen, Vuorenkoski, Valanne, & Michelsson, 1964a; 1964b) found that pediatric nurses correctly identified cry vocalization types with greater-than-chance accuracy and that female listeners who had had experience with young children attained higher cry identification accuracy scores than did inexperienced listeners. In another study Muller, Hollien and Murry (1974) used pretaped pain, hunger, and startle cries of 3–5-month-old infants, and compared the performance of mothers judging the cries of their own and unfamiliar infants. In this study the results failed to provide evidence for discriminability among cry types, and there appeared to be no differential advantage for mothers listening to cries of their own infants. Whether the discrepant findings between the studies of Wasz-Hockert and his colleagues and that of Muller et al. are attributable to differences in age of infants employed, experimental methodologies, or ethnic composition of subjects cannot as yet be determined. However several investigations have established that distinctive infant cry patterns can be objectively detected by acoustic and spectrographic analyses (Stark, Rose, & McLagen, 1975; Wasz-Hockert, Lind, Vuorenkoski, Partanen, & Valanne, 1968; Wolff, 1969).

Although it is presently unclear as to whether or not mothers can reliably discriminate the source of infant distress on the basis of auditory cues alone, there is some evidence that human mothers are at least able to discriminate between vocalizations produced by their own infants and those of others. Muller et al. (1974) found that mothers had very little difficulty in recognizing which cry samples were produced by their own child. Another study by Formby (1967) indicates that the capacity to recognize one's own infant's voice develops very early postnatally. Tape recordings of infant cries were made between 14 and 144 hours after birth; mothers listened to a series of five infants crying, including their own, and were asked to identify their own infant's cry. Twenty of the 31 mothers recognized their own infant's cry at playback times ranging from 16 to 144 hours postnatally. A second group of 10 mothers who roomed together in three- or four-bedded wards recorded the number of times they awoke to the sound of an infant crying on successive nights and how often it was the sound of their own infant that awakened them. On the first to third nights, inclusive, there were 26 wakings, of which 15 were in response to their own infants; after the fourth night, however, all but 1 of 23 wakings were for their own infants. These results suggest that mothers are capable of performing a very precise acoustical analysis, an ability that apparently develops rapidly with exposure to one's own infant. This ability may be an important one from an evolutionary point of view, ensuring specificity in the formation of the attachment bond. It is noteworthy that in the infrahuman primate species studied thus far, similar results have been noted (Itani, 1963; Klopfer, 1970; van Lawick-Goodall, 1971).

The findings of Formby (1967) have other implications with respect to caregiver–infant attachment. The fact that mothers can sleep through the crying of an infant who is not their own raises the question of whether mothers may also be able to "tune out" the cry of their own infant; such a response could conceivably occur if in the course of the infant's development qualities of the infant's crying become aversive or if the infant were unresponsive to the mother's attempts to soothe. There have been a number of recent reports on the special properties and impact of the cries of particular groups of infants. Babies identified as temperamentally "difficult" by virtue of qualities such as irregularity in biological function, slowness in adapting to new stimuli, very intense response to stimuli, and high frequency of negative-mood expression, have been described as unrewarding to care for and even as "mother killers" (Thomas & Chess, 1977; Thomas, Chess, & Birch, 1968). Bates, Bennett, and Lounsbury (1978) found that not only could these "difficult" babies be distinguished on the basis of spectrographic analyses and listener ratings of cries but also that unrelated mothers perceived the difficult babies' hunger cries to be more irritating and the babies to be more "spoiled" than the average or easy baby. Zeskind and Lester (1978) examined adults' reactions to, and the acoustic features of, the cries of neonates with prenatal and perinatal complications. These investigators found that such infant cries are discriminable from the cries of normal infants on the basis of objective acoustic criteria and that subjects listening to the high complications group rated the babies' cues as more aversive, grating, piercing, and distressing. Crying and irritability may also be involved in adults' reactions to other disorders; for example, hyperkinetic children have been reported to cry more easily (Safer & Allen, 1976) and more frequently (Cantwell, 1975).

Children with unusual-sounding cries or who are particularly irritable, fussy, and inconsolable may not only adversely affect mothers' responsiveness and subsequent development of the infant–caregiver bond, but may even precipitate abusive behavior from frustrated parents in extreme cases (Gil, 1970; Parke &

Collmer, 1975; Zeskind & Lester, 1978). Evidence that infant fussiness and irritability are factors in less-than-optimal infant–caregiver attachment comes from several sources: Moss and Robson (1968) found decreases in mother–infant attachment after the first month of postnatal life for dyads with infants who displayed sustained crying and fussing; Bell and Ainsworth (1972) indicated that there is a relationship between failure of mothers to control infant crying effectively in the early months and maternal withdrawal later on. More recently, Shaw (1977) compared the dyadic interactions of mothers of excessively crying, irritable babies with those of more temperate infants (ranging in age from 9 to 14 months) during a half-hour play session. Significant differences were found between the two groups; dyads with "criers" were found to interact less with one another and to show less overall responsiveness to one another's overtures than those with more amenable babies. With respect to the issue of child abuse, two studies have compared the psychophysiological responses of known child abusers with those of nonabusing parents to emotional stimuli involving infants. Doerr, Disbrow, and Caufield (1977) found that abusing parents showed higher heart rate levels and less habituation of heart rate and skin conductance than nonabusing parents during the viewing of emotionally laden videotaped family scenes involving children. Frodi and Lamb (1980) monitored the heart rate, skin conductance, and diastolic blood pressure of abusing and nonabusing parents as they watched videotapes of crying and smiling infants. Abusers showed greater increases in heart rate and reported more annoyance and less sympathy while viewing a crying infant. Whether these reported differences reflect differences in the premorbid personality of parents or are the product of a history of unrewarding experiences with difficult children cannot yet be determined; current theoretical formulations in the child abuse literature stress the interplay among the variables of child characteristics, parent characteristics, and environmental stressors (Parke & Collmer, 1975).

Nonetheless, the findings of the Doerr et al. (1977) the and Frodi and Lamb studies are provocative and demonstrate that physiological measures may be sensitive indices of parental response to affective stimuli from infants. Several other recent studies confirm the fact that infant signals are potent elicitors of maternal autonomic response in normal parents (e.g., Donovan, Leavitt, & Balling, 1978; Frodi, Lamb, Leavitt & Donovan, 1978; Frodi, Lamb, Leavitt, Donovan, Neff, & Sherry, 1978). In the Donovan et al. and Frodi et al., studies, however, mothers viewed or listened to affective signals produced by unfamiliar infants only. Consideration of Ainsworth's (1972) definition of attachment as an affective bond between one individual and another specific individual provokes speculation that one's own infant's signals may affect parental response in a way differing from response to an unfamiliar child. If the construct of specificity of attachment is ecologically valid, one would expect to find marked differences in response to own versus unfamiliar children, in terms of the intensity or pattern of autonomic and behavioral responses.

In our search for measures of parental sensitivity to infant signals, we have recorded psychophysiological measures and employed the sound of infant crying as our stimulus to caregivers. Our study began with an attempt to examine how parents respond autonomically and subjectively to the distress vocalizations of their own infant and one unfamiliar to them. Our goal was to examine whether psychophysiological data could help to explain how infant crying motivates caregiving by parents and others. As Dr. Lamb has suggested, in chapter 3 of this volume, one possibility is that crying functions primarily as a source of aversive stimulation to parents; the caregiver presumably ministers to the crying child in an attempt to terminate a noxious event. Murray (1979) has termed this kind of caregiving response one of *egoistic motivation*. On the other hand a caregiver's response to crying may be motivated by an empathic sharing of the infant's distress; Murray calls this kind of motivation *altruistic*. The direction of evoked heart rate response to sensory stimulation can serve as a correlative index of attentional processes (Graham & Clifton, 1966) and motivational disposition (Obrist, 1976). Hence we were interested in finding out whether parental response to their infant's crying was associated with cardiac patterns described within these paradigms. In the Graham and Clifton model heart rate acceleration has been associated with response to highly intense physical stimulation, and the acceleratory cardiac reaction is considered to reflect a pattern of environmental rejection or a *defensive response*. This defensive response pattern may also be observed with psychologically intense or aversive stimulation (Klorman, Weissberg, & Wiesenfeld, 1977). In contrast, cardiac deceleration is associated with the orienting response, which is consistent with an attentional pattern of environmental intake. Alternatively, according to Obrist's model, heart rate acceleration may be considered to reflect a process of *active coping,* and heart rate deceleration *passive coping.* Passive coping is observed in situations in which one is relatively helpless (i.e. unable to actively cope). These two conceptual models of physiological response lead to somewhat different predictions with respect to caregiver processing of infant distress signals. According to the Graham and Clifton model, a response to cries that includes cardiac deceleration may reflect orientation to a stimulus. The cry may convey specific information about the causes of an infant's distress and may therefore be useful to the caregiver in subsequent decisions about the most appropriate distress-terminating strategy to employ (e.g., picking up vs. feeding vs. ignoring). Alternatively, cardiac deceleration, according to the Obrist model, presumably reflects a "passive" motivational stance. Cardiac acceleration, on the other hand, could indicate either a defensive response, that is, a rejection of aversive stimulation (according to the Graham & Clifton model) or evidence of incipient behavioral patterns related to active coping (Obrist's model). In our work we hoped to find evidence of specific patterns of autonomic responding that reflect caregivers' motivational dispositions in response to infant cries. Hence, we felt it essential to include cries of unfamiliar infants in addition to the cries of the caregiver's own infant in order to explore any differences in motivation which may depend on the caregiver's relatedness to the infant. Infant signals are associated with differential response, and probably motivational patterns in caregivers, depending on whether the signal is produced by one's own infant or an unfamiliar infant. This fact was demonstrated in an earlier study by Wiesenfeld and Klorman (1978). In that study, silent videotaped segments of mothers' own infants' crying and smiling facial expressions produced large cardiac accelerations whereas the smiles of an unfamiliar infant evoked no significant response. The acceleratory response to the mothers' own children was interpreted as reflecting a state of excitement in parents since these smiling images were rated as highly pleasant by the subjects. In light of parallel findings in our present data, we feel that the cardiac findings in the Wiesenfeld and Klorman study could have reflected the *empathic* aspects of mothers' responses to their own infants' affective states.

In the more recent study (Wiesenfeld, Malatesta & DeLoach, 1981) we not only wanted to examine patterns of response to own versus unfamiliar infant distress signals but also to explore possible differences in parents' response to different types of cry vocalizations, namely, pain and anger, because the quality of cries related to pain has been reported to differ in acoustical morphology from those produced by frustration or hunger. Perhaps it is also true that the different cry sounds vary in terms of the specific information communicated (Wolff, 1969). For example, perhaps the specific sound of a child's anger cry produces relatively less empathy and more irritation on the part of the caregiver. This sort of finding might lead to some new insights about how particular infants with physical problems may provoke abuse from parents. An infant who communicates that he is experiencing a chronic state of discomfort may come to be viewed as a frustrated and angry child, if the parent is primarily responsive to anger he or she perceives in the infant's crying. In this case, empathic aspects of the caregiver's response may be overridden, so that the parent becomes relatively unresponsive to the child's needs or even frankly abusive in the extreme.

A second aspect of our research involved measurement of caregivers' differential ability to recognize their own infants' cries and to discriminate among a variety of cries (pain, anger, hunger, or other) on the basis of auditory cues. We asked our subjects to identify the cries as either belonging to their own infants or to another and to indicate their guess about the type of cry heard in a multiple-choice task. We also asked for subjective self-ratings of tension associated with each of the sounds, and judgments of each sound's pleasantness or unpleasantness. These ratings were included to assess any existing quantitative differences between caregivers' subjective emotional responses to the cries of their own children and those of an unfamiliar infant. We employed two types of infant cries as stimuli: anger and pain, both recorded in a previous session with the infant in our laboratory, while the mother was absent. The *anger cry* was evoked by physical restraint of the child's limbs. The *pain cry* was elicited by snapping the sole of the child's foot with a rubber band. All recorded cries were edited and stimulus tapes prepared prior to playback such that each parent heard the anger and pain cries of her own 4- to 6-month-old infant and the anger and pain cries of another, unfamiliar infant. Two tones, 400 H_z and 1000 H_z, were included as neutral stimuli as a control for the affective relevance of the infant vocalizations.

As suggested earlier, heart rate was our primary dependent autonomic measure. We also recorded skin conductance as a convergent measure in differentiating the orienting/passive coping and defensive/active coping response patterns. The six stimulus types were each presented three times in succession and arranged in four counterbalanced orders to control for response habituation over the course of the experimental session. Each sound was presented to the subject at 80dB(SPL) for a period of 15 seconds. Intertrial intervals varied randomly from 40 to 70 seconds.

Our results indicated that mothers' cardiac reaction to their children's distress cries contrasted markedly with their reactions to the unfamiliar infant's cries. Whereas the anger and pain cries of the subject's own child evoked a biphasic deceleratory–acceleratory heart rate response (Fig. 6.1), the unfamiliar child's cries elicited cardiac decelerations (Fig. 6.2). Moreover, of the two unfamiliar cry stimuli only the sound of the unfamiliar infant's pain cry was associated with a statistically significant heart rate change, whereas both of the own infant's cry types elicited significant acceleratory changes. The pain cry of the mother's own infant evoked the largest mean *skin conductance* response, surpassing reactions

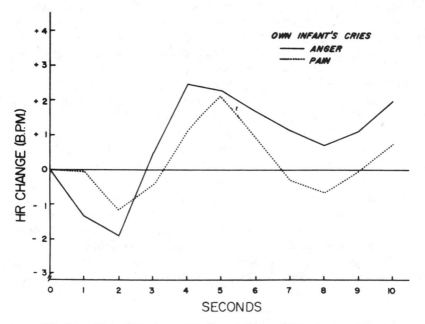

FIG. 6.1. Mothers' heart rate response to their own children's anger and pain cries over the first 10 sec of stimulation.

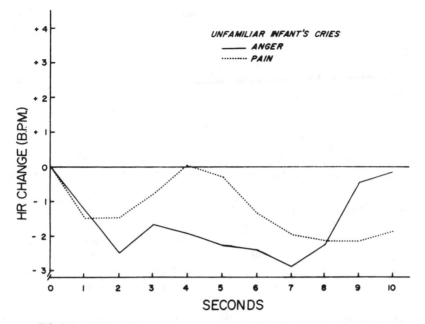

FIG. 6.2. Mothers' heart rate response to unfamiliar infants' anger and pain cries over the first 10 sec of stimulation.

to all other stimulus types, which in turn did not differ from each other. The mother's own infant's pain cry was also rated as most unpleasant indicating that this type of cry was particularly discomforting to mothers. However, except for the electrodermal response to their own children's pain cry, autonomic reactions of mothers did not differentiate between pain and anger vocalizations; that is, there were no differences found in cardiac responsiveness to the two cry types for either infant. The deceleratory cardiac response evoked by the unfamiliar child's pain cry was also found not to differ from the reactions to the two neutral tone stimuli. Hence our subjects reacted to the unfamiliar infant's cries in a manner consistent with their response to the mildly novel neutral stimuli, that is, an *orienting* response, and to their own infants' cries with a pattern consistent with a *defensive* response. Alternatively, in the terminology of Obrist, the mothers responded to the unfamiliar infant's distress in a passive-coping fashion and to their own child in a manner consistent with active coping.

There were also provocative findings regarding infant recognition and cry identification that prompted hypotheses about the cognitive process and motivational dispositions one may observe in mothers of young infants. When asked to identify tapes that were actually recordings of our subjects' own infants, the mothers were able to identify the sound as belonging to their children with near-perfect accuracy (97%) and were also quite accurate in correctly identifying the unfamiliar cries as belonging to another infant (75%). However, when errors were made in identifying infants, these errors were almost exclusively false positives, or in the language of signal detection, "false alarms." That is, mothers were much more prone to believe that the unfamiliar cries were produced by their own children (false alarm), rather than incorrectly attributing their own infants' sounds to another infant (a "miss"). We suspect that this error pattern may reflect an evolutionary bias; the second type of error, "missing," has far more serious consequences in terms of risk to the safety and security of one's own infant than does the first type.

With respect to differential response to familiar and unfamiliar infants, our most important findings appear to occur in the psychophysiological results. We interpret our findings as reflecting a specific, attachment-related response by mothers to their own infants. The mothers' own infants' cries produced markedly different autonomic responses from an unfamiliar infant's distress vocalizations and were associated with more extreme subjective emotional reactions. Another finding of interest was that mothers were able to discriminate among the cry types with significantly better-than-chance accuracy but not to the high degree found with infant recognition. In light of the finding that mothers were quite adept at recognizing their own infant in a state of distress, we believe that the mothers' autonomic patterns may reflect a disposition toward active coping when reacting to their own children's distress. Perhaps the acceleration response pattern to one's own child's distress reflects a sense of greater urgency with respect to one's own infant's negative affective expressions whereas another infant's distress requires less in the way of immediate attention; reacting to an unfamiliar infant's cries "passively" makes sense in terms of shared cultural values constraining unrelated adults from "interfering" with another person's children. The observed pattern of cardiac acceleration could also reflect a defensive response, but we hesitate to interpret such a finding as evidence that crying is primarily a noxious psychological event. This latter interpretation implies that mothers want to terminate crying for purely egoistic reasons, that is, because it is a source of aversive stimulation, which like any other noxious sound (such as the sound of an alarm clock) needs to be terminated simply because it is unpleasant. The earlier findings of the Wiesenfeld and Klorman (1978) study, as well as reflections on conversations with our subjects, suggest rather that for primary caregivers the aversiveness of the cry reflects the fact that one's own infant's distress touches an empathic core. Wiesenfeld and Klorman's finding that mothers' heart rates increased in response to the smiles of their own infants is especially difficult to reconcile with the defensive-response model. We suggest instead that the caregiver's typical reaction to crying involves a more complex cognitive-affective process than merely escaping from a source of aversive stimulation because the caregiver's relationship to that source of stimulation, one's own infant, is exceedingly more complex than to other more simple sources of aversive stimulation.

The fact that mothers rated their own infants' cries as more unpleasant than those of an unfamiliar infant, however, indicates that there is indeed some degree of aversiveness associated with hearing their infants' cries, and it would not be wise at this point to dismiss summarily the defensive response model. The relevant question becomes, "Is one's own infant's cry especially unpleasant because it is harder to ignore and therefore more aversive and noxious; or is it more unpleasant because of empathic sharing?" In our present work we attempt to tease out the components of "unpleasantness" by asking more precise questions and examine the construct of observer "empathy" by using concomitant measures.

Our data suggested that mothers' cardiac reactions did not differentiate between the pain and anger vocalizations, even of their own children. This result was at first surprising to us, in terms of our original formulations, and especially in light of the fact that mothers had demonstrated some ability to discriminate between the pain and anger sounds, as indicated by the cry-identification task. However this result is perhaps not paradoxical. The average age of the infants included in our study was 5 months; at this age infants are still quite helpless and dependent on their caregivers for attention to their needs and alleviation of discomfort. The caregivers' recognition of the infants' state of dependency may be a mitigating factor in their response to crying. Perhaps the anger cry only becomes irritating and particularly aversive to parents when it persists for an unduly long period of time and fails to be relieved by the caregiver's interventions. However, in the case of older children, angry tantrum crying is more likely to be perceived as immature and inappropriate. It thus may be fruitful to examine parental autonomic response to the crying of older children.

As a result of these data, our research interest has now become focused on two additional questions. The first is whether fathers are able to recognize their infants' vocalizations as accurately as mothers, and whether they too display differential autonomic responses to the distress states of their own and unfamiliar infants. In our latest study, involving working fathers, we have found that these fathers, unlike the mothers, did not display differential autonomic response patterns to distress signals of their own and unfamiliar infants. The fathers showed no evidence of cardiac acceleration in response to any of the distress cries whether produced by an unfamiliar child or their infant. Also the fathers' electrodermal responsivity failed to reflect differential sensitivity to their own children's pain cry as had been found with the mothers. Hence we seem to have found certain discrepancies between the reactions of mothers and their working husbands in terms of autonomic responsiveness to their own children's distress expressions.

A second question concerns the manner in which sensitivity to infant distress develops in mothers. The two areas that we are interested in exploring concern the role of prior *experience* in caregiving and *mode of feeding* (breast vs. bottle) and whether these variables are associated with differential responsivity to infant signals.

As Murray (1979) has pointed out, parity in human mothers has been associated with responsivity to infant signals. Bernal (1972) found that mothers of secondborns were less likely to ignore crying and more likely to respond promptly than were the mothers of firstborns. In an investigation of cry recognition (Wasz-Hockert et al., 1964a) it was found that female caregivers with greater experience in caregiving, as defined by parity and occupational experience (as obstetrical nurses), were more accurate in differentiating among several cry types than less experienced women. One possibility is that exposure to infants may increase the tolerability of the sound of crying and reduce the likelihood of avoidance responses among caregivers. An alternative explanation is that increased responsiveness to secondborns results from altered conceptions of the needs of infants (Murray, 1979).

These findings of apparent increased responsiveness to young infants on the part of multiparous and experienced caregivers raised the question of whether increased autonomic reactivity is associated with heightened behavioral responsiveness to infants. Relevant to the exploration of the experience factor, we combined the data for our subjects in the cry study into groups of eight primiparas and eight multiparas and averaged each group's reactions to the cries of their own infants. Figures 6.3 and 6.4 display the two groups' responses to the first trial of their own infants' anger and pain cries, respectively. These figures provide graphic illustration of the observation that multiparas tended to respond with larger heart rate accelerations than did primiparas. If this effect is borne out in subsequent investigations, it will support the notion that greater experience in rearing infants may serve to heighten caregiver sensitivity to infant signals, as defined by our autonomic measures of reactivity.

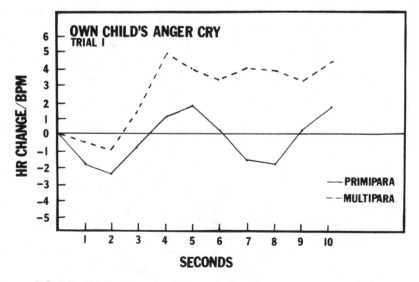

FIG. 6.3.   Primiparous and multiparous mothers' heart rate response to the first trial of their own children's anger cry over the first 10 sec of stimulation.

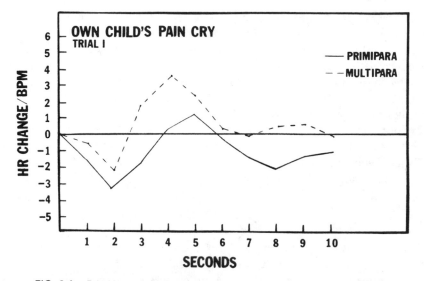

FIG. 6.4.   Primiparous and multiparous mothers' heart rate response to the first trial of their own children's pain cry over the first 10 seconds of stimulation.

We also averaged our data for 14 of our subjects who were unequivocally either breast- or bottle-feeding their infants and found that in later trials the nursing mothers were showing different patterns of response to their infants' cries than the bottle feeders, especially in response to pain cries. Of course, these comparisons are post hoc and have not been evaluated statistically; conclusive interpretation must await the results of further investigation. However there is some reason to suspect, all other factors being equal, some differences in nursing mothers' response patterns because of the kind of extended close-proximity interaction experience that characterizes breast feeding situation and because of the possibility of hormonal response priming. Our interest in exploring mode of feeding's effect on autonomic and/or behavioral sensitivity to infant signals derives from speculations within the comparative animal literature on the relative contribution of hormonal and behavioral paramenters in initiating and maintaining maternal behavior. Animal models suggest that the hormones of pregnancy prime mothers for responsiveness to infants, at least initially, but that maintenance of maternal behavior may be dependent on stimulation from the offspring (Rosenblatt, 1975). The contribution of lactogenic hormones in the regulation of maternal behavior is not yet definitively understood, and its role has been downplayed in recent literature; however, several studies using laboratory animals do suggest that lactogenic hormones facilitate maternal behavior, (Amenomori et al., 1970; Moltz et al., 1970; Rosenblatt, 1967; Zarrow et al., 1971), including response to distress signals (Beach, 1976; Newton, Peeler, & Rawlins, 1968).

Research on endocrine contributions to maternal behavior in humans is sparse, owing to the obvious obstacles to experimental research with humans and to ethical considerations as well as the widely accepted belief that human behavior is governed less by instinctual and physiological factors than is the case with infrahumans. Research focused on this issue may disclose effects with important implications for theoretical models of maternal behavior. The physiological monitoring of maternal arousal in response to infant signals as a function of hormonal state (breast- or bottle-feeding) is a unique and potentially sensitive means of assessing differential responsivity in the context of naturally occurring hormonal state differences. The post hoc analyses of our data encourage us to examine physiological and psychological concomitants of feeding mode further.

SUMMARY

In conclusion, we are exploring enthusiastically the potential of psychophysiological indices of caregivers' responsivity to their own infants' affective expressions as a means of assessing individual differences in sensitivity to infants. On the basis of two investigations that utilized visual and auditory stimulation it was found that mothers' characteristic autonomic response to their own infants' crying includes an acceleration of heart rate. In response to an unfamiliar infant's expressions, the cardiac response was deceleratory. In addition, because mothers were found to be highly accurate in recognizing their own infants' cries, we feel that combined autonomic and signal detection data can be utilized to compare groups of caregivers or others who may differ because of demographic, experiential, and personality characteristics. For example, as mentioned earlier, one personality attribute that is of particular interest to us is the level of caregiver empathy and how this factor may relate to specific sensitivity to infant affective states. The ability of a caregiver to recognize, share, or understand a child's emotional state on the basis of preverbal or nonverbal cues is undoubtedly implicated in sensitive caregiving and most likely in the child's social and emotional development. It has also become clear that individual differences also exist among infants in terms of cry quality and intensity and other temperamental attributes such as soothability as well as obvious differences such as sex and birth status (full-term vs. premature). It is not unreasonable to expect that these characteristics will also be found to affect caregivers' responses to infants. Our hope is that such work will lead us to some data-based conclusions about necessary and sufficient components of an optimal early environment and how we may promote these in individual dyads.

REFERENCES

Ainsworth, M. D. S. Object relations, dependency, and attachment: A theoretical review of the mother–infant relationship. *Child Development,* 1969, *40,* 969–1025.

Ainsworth, M. D. S. Attachment and dependency: A comparison. In J. Gewirtz (Ed.), *Attachment and Dependency*. Washington, D.C.: Winston, 1972.

Aldrich, C., Sung, C., & Knopp, C. The crying of newly born babies: II. The individual phase. *Journal of Pediatrics*, 1945, *27*, 89–96.

Amenomori, Y., Chen, C. L., & Meites, J. Serum prolactin levels in rats during different reproductive states. *Endocrinology*, 1970, *86*, 506–510.

Bates, J. E., Bennett, C. A., & Lounsbury, M. L. Temperamental difficulties in infants: Correlates of maternal perceptions. A paper presented at International Conference on Infant Studies, Providence, R.I., March, 1978.

Beach, F. A. Hormonal control of sex-related behavior. In F. A. Beach (Ed.), *Human Sexuality in Four Perspectives*. Baltimore: Johns Hopkins University Press, 1976.

Bell, S. M., & Ainsworth, M. D. S. Infant crying and maternal responsiveness. *Child Development*, 1972, *43*, 1171–1190.

Bernal, J. Crying during the first 10 days of life and maternal responses. *Developmental Medicine and Child Neurology*, 1972, *14*, 362–372.

Bowlby, J. *Attachment and loss: Vol. 1. Attachment*. New York: Basic Books, 1969.

Cantwell, P. P. *The hyperactive child: Diagnosis, management, current research*. New York: Spectrum, 1975.

Doerr, H., Disbrow, M., & Caufield, C. *Psychophysiological response patterns in child abusers*. Paper presented at the annual meeting of the Society for Psychophysiological Research, Philadelphia, October 1977.

Donovan, W. L., & Leavitt, L. A. Early cognitive development and its relation to maternal physiologic and behavioral responsiveness. *Child Development*, 1978, *49*, 1251–1254.

Donovan, W. L., Leavitt, L. A., & Balling, J. D. Maternal physiological response to infant signals. *Psychophysiology*, 1978, *15*, 68–74.

Epple, G. Comparative studies on vocalization in marmoset monkeys (*Hapalidae*). *Folia Primatologia*, 1968, *8*, 1–40.

Epple, G. Parental behavior in *Saguinus fuscicollis ssp* (*Callithricidae*). *Folia Primatologia*, 1975, *24*, 221–238.

Field, T. Maternal stimulation during infant feeding. *Developmental Psychology*, 1977, *13*, 539–540.

Formby, D. Maternal recognition of infant's cry. *Developmental Medicine and Child Neurology*, 1967, *9*, 293–298.

Frodi, A., & Lamb, M. Child abusers' responses to infant smiles and cries. *Child Development*, 1980, *51*, 238–241.

Frodi, A., Lamb, M., Leavitt, L., & Donovan, W. Fathers' and mothers' responses to infant smiles and cries. *Infant Behavior and Development*, 1978, *1*, 187–198.

Frodi, A. M., Lamb, M. E. Leavitt, L. A., Donovan, W. L., Neff, C. & Sherry, D. Fathers' and mothers' responses to the faces and cries of normal and premature infants. *Developmental Psychology*, 1978, *14*, 490–498.

Gil, D. *Violence against children: Physical child abuse in the United States*. Cambridge, Mass.: Harvard University Press, 1970.

Graham, F. K., & Clifton, R. K. Heart-rate change as a component of the orienting response. *Psychological Bulletin*, 1966, *65*, 305–320.

Itani, J. Vocal communication of the wild Japanese monkey. *Primates*, 1963, *4*, 11–66.

Klopfer, P. H. Discrimination of young in Galagos. *Folia Primatologia*, 1970, *13*, 137–143.

Klorman, E., Weissberg, R., & Wiesenfeld, A. Individual differences in fear and autonomic reactions to affective stimulation. *Psychophysiology*. 1977, *14*, 45–51.

Kuhn, J. J. Progesterone withdrawal as the lactogenic trigger in the rat. *Journal of Endocrinology*, 1969, *44*, 39–54.

Lawick-Goodall, J. van The behavior of free-living chimpanzees in the Gombe stream reserve. *Animal Behavior Monographs*, 1968, *1*, 161–300.

Lawick-Goodall, J. van *The Shadow of Man*. Boston: Houghton Mifflin, 1971.

Moltz, H., Lubin, M., Leon, M., & Numan, M. Hormonal induction of maternal behavior in the ovariectomized nulliparous rat. *Physiology and Behavior*, 1970, *5*, 1371-1377.

Moss, H., & Robson, K. *The role of protest behavior in the development of mother-infant attachment*. Paper presented at the meeting of the American Psychological Association, September 1968.

Muller, E., Hollien, H., & Murry, T. Perceptual responses to infant crying: Identification of cry types. *Journal of Child Language*, 1974, *1*, 89-95.

Murray, A. Infant crying as an elicitor of parental behavior: An examination of two models. *Psychological Bulletin*, 1979, *86*, 191-215.

Newton, N., Peeler, D., & Rawlins, C. Effect of lactation on maternal behavior in mice with comparative data on humans. *Lying-In: Journal of Reproductive Medicine*, 1968, *1*, 257-262.

Obrist, P. The cardiovascular-behavioral interaction-as it appears today. *Psychophysiology*, 1976, *13*, 95-107.

Ostwald, P. The sounds of infancy. *Developmental Medicine and Child Neurology*, 1972, *14*, 350-361.

Parke, R., & Collmer, C. Child abuse: An interdisciplinary review. In E. M. Hetherington (Ed.), *Review of child development research* (Vol. 5). Chicago: University of Chicago Press, 1975.

Redican, W. K. Facial expression in nonhuman primates. In L. A. Rosenblum (Ed.) *Primate behavior: Developments in field and laboratory research*. New York: Academic Press, 1975.

Rosenblatt, J. S. Nonhormonal basis of maternal behavior in the rat. *Science*, 1975, *156*, 1512-1514.

Rosenblatt, J. S. Prepartum and postpartum regulation of maternal behavior in the rat, parent-infant interaction, *Ciba Foundation Symposium 33*. Amsterdam: ASP (Elsevier).

Safer, D. J., & Allen, R. P. *Hyperactive children: Diagnosis and management*. Baltimore: University Park Press, 1976.

Shaw, C. A comparison of the patterns of mother-baby interaction for a group of crying, irritable babies and a group of more amenable babies. *Child Care Health and Development*, 1977, *3*, 1-12.

Sherman, M. The differentiation of emotional responses in infants: I. Judgments of emotional responses from motion picture views and from actual observation. *Journal of Comparative Psychology*, 1927, *7*, 265-284. (a)

Sherman, M. The differentiation of emotional responses in infants: II. The ability of observers to judge the emotional characteristics of the crying of infants, and the voice of an adult. *Journal of Comparative Psychology*, 1927, *7*, 335-351. (b)

Siegel, H., & Rosenblatt, J. S. Hormonal basis of hysterectomy-induced maternal behavior during pregnancy in the rat. *Hormone & Behavior*, 1975, *6*, 211-222.

Stark, R., Rose, S., & McLagen, M. Features of infant sounds: The first eight weeks of life. *Journal of Child Language*, 1975, *2*, 205-221.

Takeda, R. Development of vocal communication in man-raised Japanese monkeys. *Primates*, 1965, *6*, 337-380.

Thomas, A., & Chess, S. *Temperament and Development*. New York: Brunner/Mazel, 1977.

Thomas A., Chess, S., & Birch, J. *Temperament and behavior disorders in children*. New York: New York University Press, 1968.

Wasz-Hockert, O., Lind, J., Vuorenkoski, V., Partanen, Y., & Valanne, E. The infant cry: A spectrographic and auditory analysis. Clinics in Developmental Medicine, #29., Spastics International Medical Publications, 1968, 1-41.

Wasz-Hockert, O., Partanen, T. S., Vuorenkoski, V., Valanne, E. H., & Michelsson, K. Effect of training on ability to identify pre-verbal vocalizations. *Developmental Medicine and Child Neurology*, 1964, *6*, 393-402. (a)

Wasz-Hockert, O., Partanen, T. S., Vuorenkoski, V., Valanne, E. H., & Michelsson, K. Identification of specific meaning in infant vocalization. *Experientia*, 1964, *20*, 154-5. (b)

Wiesenfeld, A., & Klorman, R. The mother's psychophysiological reactions to contrasting affective expressions by her own and an unfamiliar infant. *Developmental Psychology,* 1978, *14,* 294-304.

Wiesenfeld, A. R., Malatesta, C. Z. & DeLoach, L. Differential parental response to familiar and unfamiliar infant distress signals, *Infant Behavior and Development,* 1981, *4,* in press.

Wolff, P. The natural history of crying and other vocalizations in early infancy. In B. Foss (Ed.), *Determinants of infant behavior* (Vol. 4). London: Methuen, 1969.

Zarrow, M. X., Gandelman, R., & Denenberg, V. H. Prolactin: Is it an essential hormone for maternal behavior in the mammal? *Hormones & Behavior,* 1971, *2,* 343-354.

Zeskind, S., & Lester, B. Acoustic features and auditory perceptions of the cries of newborns with prenatal and perinatal complications. *Child Development,* 1978, *49,* 580-589.

7 On How the Rat Mother Defends Her Young Against Enteric Infection

Howard Moltz
University of Chicago

Under certain conditions both the human and the rat neonate are susceptible to necrotizing enterocolitis, an often fatal disease of the gastrointestinal tract. In each species the symptomatology is the same: delayed gastric emptying, abdominal distension, enteric bleeding, perforation of the ileum and colon, and finally overwhelming sepsis and death. The microorganism most often implicated in the etiology of this disease is *Escherichia coli,* a gram-negative aerobe. But although *E. coli* is pathogenic, it normally inhabits the mammalian gut (e.g., Bell, Feigin, Ternberg, & Brotherton, 1978), which raises the question of why mammals, young and old alike, are not chronically afflicted with necrotizing enterocolitis? Obviously because there are protective mechanisms at work. The identity of some of these mechanisms, in the rat at least, is the subject of the present chapter.

THE ROLE OF MATERNAL MILK

The gastrointestinal tract of the rat, although sterile at birth, quickly becomes colonized by a variety of flora. This colonization does not involve the stomach nor the proximal small intestine, but it does involve the ileum and, in particular, the cecum and colon (Donaldson, 1964). Against such colonization and the pathogenic organisms that colonization brings, the rat is born largely defenseless (Humphrey & White, 1970). What must the young rat do to guard selected regions of its gut against *E. coli* and other bacteria potentially as dangerous? The answer is deceptively simple: It must drink its mother's milk.

   Rat milk, and indeed the milk of all mammalian species, contains protective agents that provide the gut with its own immune system, distinct from the general or systemic immune system (e.g., Goldman & Smith, 1973; Shearman, Parkin, & McClelland, 1972; South, 1971; Stechschulte & Austen, 1970). These agents are varied and include a class of antibodies known as secretory immunoglobulins; an iron-binding protein, lactoferrin, which inhibits the growth of en-teropathogenic bacteria; leukocytes, especially macrophages, that function phagocytically; and a bifidobacterium that synthesizes lactic and acetic acid, thereby lowering the pH of the gut and creating an environment inimical to the growth of E. coli.

To promote bacterial invasion of the large intestine Barlow and her associates (Barlow & Santulli, 1975; Barlow, Santulli, Heird, Pitt, Blanc, & Schullinger, 1974; Pitt, Barlow, & Heird, 1977) induced enteric ischemia in newborn pups by hypoxia or in some instances by cold stress. They found that necrotizing en-terocolitis and death rapidly ensued in such ischemic-induced pups if they were maintained on artificial formula (Similac PM 60/40 supplemented with EsBilac). If they were fed mother's milk, however, even for a period as brief as 24 hours following birth, they remained healthy. It is evident that the bacteriocidal and the bacteriostatic agents contained in milk provide the neonatal rat with an enteric

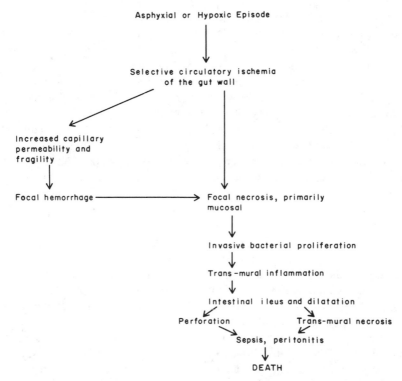

FIG. 7.1.   Probable course of events leading to necrotizing enterocolitis in the neonate. Adapted from Touloukian et al., 1972.

immune system that functions capably even under conditions of stress-induced ischemia.

The use of cold or hypoxia in the experiments just cited points to an important parameter in the etiology of necrotizing enterocolitis, namely, stress. When a mammal is stressed, cardiac output is reflexively shunted away from the mesenteric vascular bed to the heart and brain. This spontaneous redistribution of blood, with the ischemia it produces in the gut wall, makes the mucosa of the gut susceptible to bacterial adherence and subsequent bacterial proliferation (McNeish, Fleming, Turner, & Evans, 1975; Touloukian, Posch, & Spencer, 1972). Without benefit of the local immune system established through the ingestion of maternal milk such bacterial proliferation soon leads to an invasion of intestinal tissue and, in most instances, to the events that characterize necrotizing enterocolitis. Figure 7.1 illustrates these events graphically.

THE ROLE OF MATERNAL FECES

The rat pup of course does not remain on an exclusive diet of maternal milk. At about 14 days, some 2 weeks before it is weaned, it begins to ingest solid food. At that age it also begins to respond to a pheromone in the mother's feces (Leon & Moltz, 1971, 1972). These two events—the ingestion of solid food and the attraction to a fecally contained pheromone—are closely related in time, and a question arises as to what this relationship reflects. It may, of course, reflect nothing more than simple coincidence. On the other hand, it may reflect an important physiological linkage.

The ingestion of solid food brings about a marked increase in the bacterial population of the gut, imposing a new challenge on a gastrointestinal immune system heretofore supported by maternal milk alone (Donaldson, 1964; Mata & Urrutia, 1971). Perhaps the pup meets this new challenge by responding first to a pheromone in the mother's feces and then by actually consuming those feces. If such feces contain an agent that raises the immunocompetence of the gut, enabling the pup to meet the food-induced escalation of intestinal bacteria, then the adaptive value of its pheromone-seeking behavior would be obvious.

Of course such a hypothetical sequence of events poses many questions. Does the pup typically ingest maternal feces? If it does, then is such consumption prompted by the antigenic challenge of solid food? Moreover, if preweanling young, 14 days and older, are stressed and at the same time denied access to maternal feces, will they be prone to gastrointestinal infection? And finally, and most important, what might the mother's feces contain that could conceivably protect her young against the often-lethal disease we have been calling necrotizing enterocolitis?

First, do rat pups typically ingest maternal feces? We do know that they do at 20 days of age (Leon, 1974), but we do not know that they do either earlier or later in the preweanling period. Sarah Kilpatrick, working in the author's laboratory, is trying to find the answer. She is feeding lactating females a dye called Eosin 7, a dye that distinctively colors the feces of the mother while leaving her milk unaffected. Preliminary data, obtained by examining the contents of the pup's gut, indicate that maternal feces are first ingested at 14 days of age and that they cease to be ingested at approximately 30 days of age. It is at 14 days, of course, that pups begin to consume solid food, and it is at approximately 27–30 days that they leave the nipple.

If the ingestion of maternal feces occurs in response to an increase in intestinal bacteria brought about by the intake of solid food, then we might expect that pups maintained on an exclusive diet of milk would neither respond to the pheromone nor consume pheromone-containing feces. We should expect also that if preweanling pups are given access to food but not to maternal feces, then either cold stress or hypoxia would result in an increase in the incidence of enteric disease. With reference to the latter expectation, Theresa Lee, also working in the author's laboratory, has constructed a "tail-cup." This tail-cup, as the name implies, consists of a small plastic container that is attached to the proximal end of the tail by means of a rubber sleeve (Barnes, 1962; Barnes & Fiala, 1959; Barnes, Fiala, McGehee, & Brown, 1957). Such tail-cups that have been fitted have thus far prevented pups from ingesting maternal feces. The next step, of course, is to stress these fecally deprived pups and look for signs of necrotizing enterocolitis.

As already mentioned, the most important question confronting us is the question of just what the maternal female might excrete in her feces to protect her young against enteric infection. Perhaps the answer is to be found in the events surrounding pheromonal emission.

The pheromone to which we refer is carried in the feces not only of the lactating female but also in the feces of the nulliparous female that has been induced to behave maternally through continuous association with young (Leidahl & Moltz, 1975, 1977). In both, the pheromone is released initially 14 days after the onset of maternal behavior, and it ceases to be released at approximately 27 days (Leidahl & Moltz, 1975). The pups, for their part, begin responding to the pheromone at 14 days postpartum and, in synchrony with the mother, they cease to respond at approximately 27 days postpartum (Moltz, Leidahl, & Rowland, 1974; Moltz & Leon, 1973).

We know that prolactin is essential for the release of the pheromone, but adrenal and ovarian hormones are not (Leidahl & Moltz, 1977; Leon & Moltz, 1973). We know also that prolactin is characteristically elevated during the two-week period immediately preceding pheromonal emission in both the lactating female and the maternally behaving nulliparous female as well (Amenomori, Chen, & Meites, 1970; Marinari & Moltz, 1978).

Although the pheromone is prolactin dependent, it is not lactation dependent because the maternally behaving nulliparous female—which of course does not lactate—nonetheless emits the pheromone. In contrast the male does not emit the attractant even when he is behaving as maternally as his nulliparous counterpart and indeed even when he is castrated and injected with prolactin (Leidahl & Moltz, 1975). Only after repeated intracecal injections of bile, bile drawn from pheromone-emitting females, will the male release the pheromone. And in such males neither castration nor exogenous prolactin is necessary (Moltz & Leidahl, 1977).

What Might the Pheromone Be?

The pheromone-emitting females just referred to had been lactating for 21 days. This fact is important because the same amount of bile drawn from females lactating for only 5 days (and which, as a consequence, were not emitting the pheromone) failed to promote pheromonal emission in the male. Evidently the composition of bile was altered between 5 and 21 days of lactation, altered in a way that made it pheromone inducing. It is unlikely that this alteration involved a change in total bile-acid concentration, because the overall concentration of bile acids does not change significantly from the nonpregnant to the lactating state, nor does it change during the course of lactation (Kilpatrick & Moltz, unpublished data; Klaasen & Strom, 1978). Rather what we think we are dealing with is an alteration in the ratio of one primary bile acid to another, specifically, an alteration in the ratio of cholic acid to chenodeoxycholic acid.

As is well known, the major primary bile acids of the rat are cholic acid and chenodeoxycholic acid. Conjugation by peptide linkage occurs with taurine and glycine, respectively, to yield the corresponding tauro- and glyco- acids. These conjugated acids enter the small intestine where, at the terminal ileum, they are largely reabsorbed into the enterohepatic circulation. What fraction escapes into the cecum is deconjugated and dehydroxylated by intestinal microflora to form the secondary bile acids, deoxycholic acid from cholic acid and lithocholic acid from chenodeoxycholic acid (Bergstrom & Norman, 1953; Gustafsson, Bergstrom, Lindstedt, & Norman, 1957; Haslewood, 1964; Norman & Sjovall, 1958).

The secondary bile acids also contribute to the enterohepatic circulation through passive diffusion from the cecum and colon (Weiner & Lack, 1968). However they do so differentially. Lithocholic acid, being of low polarity and low solubility, is poorly reabsorbed from the large intestine (Gustafsson & Norman, 1962; Norman & Sjovall, 1960) whereas deoxycholic acid, in contrast, is readily reabsorbed (Heaton, 1972; Lindstedt & Samuelsson, 1959; Mekhjian & Phillips, 1970; Norman & Sjovall, 1958(a); 1958(b); Olivecrona & Sjovall, 1959).

Relevant to this discussion of bile acids, and particularly to the efficiency with which deoxycholic acid re-enters the enterohepatic circulation, are two recent discoveries (Leon, 1974). The first is that the pheromone is synthesized in the cecum; the second is that the cecum of the adult male normally contains the pheromone. The latter has been established by taking material directly from the ceca of adult males and demonstrating that it strongly attracts young. That such young are not attracted at all to the anal excreta of these same adult males suggests that, although the pheromone is always present in the cecum, it typically fails to survive passage through the colon. Two questions then become relevant: What is it that is lost in the colon, and why can the female overcome this loss when the male cannot?

What might well be lost in colonic passage is deoxycholic acid, which is *not* to suggest that the pheromone is deoxycholic acid, and deoxycholic acid alone. A pheromone, most often, is constituted by a number of different compounds, rarely by a single compound (Beauchamp, Doty, Moulton, & Mugford, 1976). Rather what we are suggesting is that the maternal pheromone, whatever its full chemical composition, has deoxycholic acid as an essential moiety. The question of why females overcome the loss of deoxycholic acid under certain conditions and so emit the pheromone, when males do not, relates to sex differences in prolactin binding by the liver.

We know from the research of Posner and his colleagues (Posner, Kelly, & Friesen, 1974, 1975; Posner, Kelly, Shiu, & Friesen, 1974) and from the more recent work of Manni, Chambers, & Pearson (1978) that the prolactin induces its own receptors at the liver, which is to say that the liver responds to an increase in circulating prolactin by forming additional binding sites to take up the peptide. There is, however, a male–female difference in this liver responsiveness, the male liver showing a substantially lower capacity to form new prolactin receptors than the female liver (Costlow, Buschow, & McGuire, 1975; Kelly, LeBlanc, Ferland, Labrie, & DeLean, 1977). The result is that the male liver, having fewer prolactin receptors than the female liver, recognizes less of the hormone and so takes up less.

In brief we think that the maternally behaving female, as a consequence of her high hepatic binding of prolactin, comes to synthesize cholic acid in greater-than-normal amounts, enabling a critical fraction of the cholic metabolite, deoxycholic acid, to show up in her anal excreta. It is this fraction in combination with other compounds contained in the fecal material that constitutes the pheromone, attracting young. That the male characteristically forms fewer hepatic prolactin receptors than the female and so presumably experiences little or no change in the output of deoxycholic acid would explain why the male, although capable of releasing the pheromone in response to bile drawn from a pheromone-emitting female, cannot do so endogenously. Figure 7.2 displays graphically the proposed mechanism of pheromonal emission.

Two experiments that relate to Fig. 7.2 are currently underway in the author's laboratory. The first, utilizing thin layer chromatography, is designed to determine what changes, if any, occur in the ratio of the primary bile acids during the course of lactation. We expect, of course, to find an increase in cholic acid

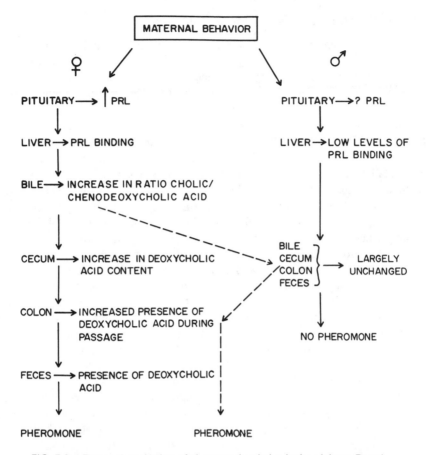

FIG. 7.2.   Proposed mechanism of pheromonal emission in the adult rat. Dotted arrows: bile, drawn from a pheromone-emitting female, injected into the cecum of an adult male. PRL: prolactin.

relative to chenodeoxycholic acid and, consequently, an increase in the absolute amount of deoxycholic acid.

The second experiment that is underway is designed to determine whether the male can be made pheromone-emitting and the female nonemitting through perinatal alteration of gonadal hormones. It is well known that many sexually dimorphic characteristics of the rat can be changed by manipulation of sex steroids during critical periods of early development. Because the hepatic binding of prolactin is sexually dimorphic, perhaps it too is susceptible to the same change. Thus by castrating neonatal males and by "androgenizing" neonatal females, we may be able to reverse the typical male–female difference in pheromonal emission. (The two experiments just sketched are being carried out by Sarah Kilpatrick.)

Enteric Infection and Deoxycholic Acid

It has already been mentioned that necrotizing enterocolitis has an etiology that involves such common gram-negative organisms as *E. coli*. Evidence that deoxycholic acid within the large intestine protects against the endotoxin of *E. coli*, and thus against such enterotoxemic conditions as necrotizing enterocolitis, is quite compelling: (1) When the endotoxin of *E. coli* was extracted with phenol and treated with sodium deoxycholate, the toxic units were split into smaller, nonpyrogenic structural elements (Rudbach, Anacker, Haskins, Johnson, Milner, & Ribi, 1966); (2) When the endotoxin was incubated with sodium deoxycholate and administered parenterally, no pathological effects were seen; without prior incubation overwhelming sepsis occurred (Bertok, 1977; Kocsar, Bertok, & Varteresz, 1969); (3) When the *E. coli* endotoxin was administered orally to intact rats in dosages 500–3000 times the parenterally lethal dose, the animal remained asymptomatic; however when the bile duct was cannulated to prevent bile from reaching the gastrointestinal tract, oral administration rapidly resulted in death (Berczi, Bertok, Baintner, & Veress, 1968; Bertok, 1977).

It seems clear that deoxycholic acid defends against *E. coli* by rendering its endotoxin harmless. The defense is what Bertok (1977) called "physico-chemical," based on the capacity of the bile acid to fragment the endotoxin molecule through detergent action. Following from this demonstrated detergent action is the hypothesis that response to the maternal pheromone, in leading to the ingestion of feces containing deoxycholic acid, confers protection against the potentially pathogenic effects of enteric *E. coli*.

Of course, if pups between 14 and 27 days of age have a deoxycholic-acid profile similar to that of the adult, then it would be difficult to see what measure of protection would be conferred by ingesting still more deoxycholic acid through maternal feces. That such pups in fact are strikingly deficient not only in deoxycholic acid but in other bile acids as well was demonstrated recently by Barth and his associates (Barth, Zaumseil, & Klinger, 1977). They showed that the secretion of the dihydroxy bile acids, of which deoxycholic is one, increased eight-fold between the 10th and 30th day of life, while the trihydroxy acid (cholic) increased twofold. It is very much to the point that adult levels of these bile acids are attained at 30 days of age, approximately the age at which pups stop responding to the pheromone. Figure 7.3 illustrates the proposed mechanism of pup responsiveness.

One experiment suggested by Fig. 7.3 is obvious and involves pups that are periodically stressed and are not permitted access to maternal feces. The question is will feeding deoxycholic acid protect such pups against enteric infection?

A second and perhaps less obvious experiment relates to the question of whether responsiveness to maternal feces can be manipulated by altering the bile profile of the developing pup. Specifically will a pup ingesting laboratory pellets supplemented with deoxycholic acid cease responding to maternal feces prior to the usual age of 27 days, or will it fail perhaps to respond altogether? The answer

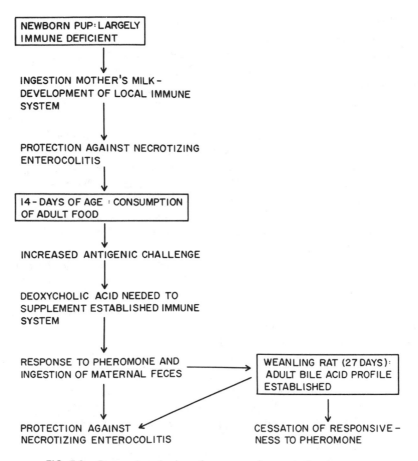

FIG. 7.3. Proposed mechanism of pup responsiveness to the pheromone.

might provide some clue as to what preweanling young find so attractive in the feces of their mother.

But what of the mother; how attracted is she to the feces of her young? It is well known that she vigorously licks the perineal region of her pups and that this licking promotes defecation. The assumption is that the mother consumes this fecal material, and the assumption is correct. Theresa Lee fed dye to 13-day-old young and found the coloring material throughout the gastrointestinal tract of the mother. Ms. Lee then asked whether the synchrony between pheromonal release on the part of the mother and pheromonal responsiveness on the part of the young is entirely fortuitous or whether the pups themselves exert some measure of control over pheromonal release. In pursuit of this question, Ms. Lee discovered that mothers that had been lactating for 18 days but who, through litter substitution were caring for pups 10 days of age, did not emit the attractant. Evidently such 10-day-old pups inhibited emission in their foster mothers, that is, in females who had been lactating for a period of time sufficient to have had an oversupply of deoxycholic acid in their ceca and so were releasing the pheromone. Perhaps the inhibition exerted by these experimental pups was conveyed through their feces.

Rat young, 10 days of age, are on a diet that consists exclusively of milk. Because such a diet has a high presence of *Bifidobacterium bifidum,* substantial levels of acidic and lactic acid are produced in the gut, making the feces of course quite acidic. Might the ingestion of such feces by a mother lactating for 18 days change the pH of her gut to inhibit the very microflora she needs to convert cholic acid to deoxycholic acid? If it does, then although she may have established a sufficient number of prolactin binding sites at the liver and as a consequence may be producing high levels of cholic acid, she may still be deficient in deoxycholic acid. Perhaps it is only when her pups begin to ingest solid food that this deficiency is corrected.

We think of the ingestion of solid food as bringing about a decrease in the population of milk-borne, acid-forming bacteria in the pup's gut and with it an increase in the alkalinity of its feces. As a consequence, in ingesting such feces, the mother comes to ingest a new "kind" of pup excreta—excreta that, by increasing the pH of her own gut, "lifts" from acidic suppression those bacteria she normally uses to deconjugate and dehydroxylate cholic acid to deoxycholic acid. Only then will she presumably release the pheromone. But of course we do not know whether this hypothetical sequence of events actually takes place, that is, wehther the pup influences the pH of the mother's gut, and hence the composition of her bile, through the pH of its own feces. However if the pup does so, then we would be able to understand how mother and young manage to become so finely attuned at a pheromonal level.

In conclusion I want to acknowledge an obvious fact, namely, that my presentation has been "long" on speculation and rather "short" on data. But along with that acknowledgment, I want to express the hope that by the time the next symposium is held on *Parental Behavior: Its Causes and Consequences* I shall have reversed the balance. We, (my graduate students and I) are certainly working in that direction.

ACKNOWLEDGMENTS

The author's research is currently supported by NIH Grant HD-06872. It is not only an obligation but a pleasure to acknowledge the comments and ideas of my graduate students, Sarah Kilpatrick and Theresa Lee.

REFERENCES

Amenomori, Y., C. L. Chen, & Meites, J. Serum prolactin levels in rats during different reproductive states. *Endocrinology,* 1970, *70,* 506–510.

Barlow, B., & Santulli, T. V. Importance of multiple episodes of hypoxia or cold stress on the development of enterocolitis in an animal model. *Surgery,* 1975, *77,* 687–690.

Barlow, B., Santulli, T. V., Heird, W. C., Pitt, J., Blanc, W. A., & Schullinger, J. N. An experimental study of acute neonatal enterocolitis—the importance of breast milk. *Journal of Pediatric Surgery,* 1974, *9,* 587–594.

Barnes, R. H. Nutritional implications of coprophagy. *Nutrition Review,* 1962, *20,* 289–291.

Barnes, R. H., & Fiala, G. Effects of the prevention of coprophagy in the rat. VI. Vitamin K. *Journal of Nutrition,* 1959, *68,* 603–614.

Barnes, R. H., Fiala, G., McGehee, B., & Brown, A. Prevention of coprophagy in the rat. *Journal of Nutrition,* 1957, *63,* 489–498.

Barth, A., Zaumseil, J., & Klinger, W. Gallenflusse und Gallensaureausscheidung bei mannlichen Wistarratten (Jena) verschiedenen Alters. *Zeitschrift Versuchstierk,* 1977, *19,* 26–35.

Beauchamp, G. K., Doty, R. L., Moulton, D. G., & Mugford, R. A. The pheromone concept in mammalian chemical communication: A critique. In R. L. Doty, (Ed). *Mammalian Olfaction, Reproductive Processes, and Behavior.* New York: Academic Press, 1976.

Bell, M. J., Feigin, R. D., Ternberg, J. L., & Brotherton, T. Evaluation of gastrointestinal microflora in necrotizing enterocolitis. *Journal of Pediatrics,* 1978, *92,* 589–592.

Berczi, J., Bertok, L., Baintner, K., & Veress, B. Failure of oral *Escherichia coli* endotoxin to induce either tolerance or toxic symptoms in rats. *Journal Pathological Bacteriology* 1968, *96,* 481–486.

Bergstrom, S., & Norman, A. Metabolic products of cholesterol in bile and feces of rats. *Proceedings of the Society Experimental Biology and Medicine* 1953, *83,* 71–74.

Bertok, L. Physico-chemical defense of vertebrate organisms: The role of bile acids in defense against bacterial endotoxins. *Perspectives in Biology and Medicine 21*: 70–76, 1977.

Costlow, M. E., Buschow, R. A., & McGuire, W. L. Prolactin stimulation of prolactin receptors in rat liver. *Life Sciences 17*: 1457–1466, 1975.

Donaldson, R. M. Normal bacterial populations of the intestine and their relation to intestinal function. *New England Journal of Medicine,* 1964, *270,* 938–945, 994–1000, 1050–1056.

Goldman, A. S., & Smith, C. W. Host resistance factors in human milk. *Journal of Pediatrics,* 1973, *82,* 1082–1090.

Gustafsson, B. E., Bergstrom, S., Lindstedt, S., & Norman, A. Turnover and nature of fecal bile acids in germ-free and infected rats fed cholic $-24-^{14}C$. *Proceedings of the Society of experimental Biology and Medicine, 94,* 1957, 467–471.

Gustafsson, B. E., & Norman, A. Comparison of bile acids in intestinal contents in germ-free and conventional rats. *Proceedings of the Society of experimental Biology and Medicine 110:* 1962, 387–389.

Haslewood, G. A. The biological significance of chemical differences in bile salts. *Biological Review* 1964, *39,* 537–574.

Heaton, K. W. *Bile salts in health and disease.* London: Churchill Livingstone, 1972.

Humphrey, J. H., & White, R. G. *Immunology for students of medicine.* London: Oxford University Press, 1970.

Kelly, P. A., LeBlanc, G., Ferland, L., Labrie, F., & DeLean, A. Androgen inhibition of basal and estrogen-stimulated prolactin binding in rat liver. *Molecular and cellular Endocrinology* 1977, *9,* 195–204.

Klaasen, C. D., & Strom, S. C. Comparison of biliary excretory function and bile composition in male, female, and lactating female rats. *Drug Metabolism and Disposition* 1978, *6,* 120–124.

Kocsar, L. T., Bertok, L., & Varteresz, V. Effect of bile acids on the intestinal absorption of endotoxin in rats. *Journal of Bacteriology,* 1969, *100,* 220–223.

Leidahl, L. C., & Moltz, H. Emission of the maternal pheromone in the nulliparous female and failure of emission in the adult male. *Physiology and Behavior* 1975, *14,* 421–424.

Leidahl, L. C., & Moltz, H. Emission of the maternal pheromone in nulliparous and lactating females. *Physiology and Behavior,* 1977, *18,* 399–402.

Leon, M. Maternal Pheromone. *Physiology and Behavior*, 1974, *13*, 441-453.

Leon, M., & Moltz, H. Maternal pheromone: Discrimination by preweanling albino rats. *Physiology and Behavior*, 1971, *7*, 265-267.

Leon, M., & Moltz, H. The development of the pheromonal bond in the albino rat. *Physiology and Behavior*. 1972, *8*, 683-686.

Leon, M., & Moltz, H. Endocrine control of pheromonal emission in the postpartum rat. *Physiology and Behavior*, 1973, *10*, 65-67.

Lindstedt, S., & Samuelsson, B. Bile acids and steroids: On the interconversion of cholic and deoxycholic acid in the rat. *Journal of Biological Chemistry*, 1959, *234*, 2026-2030.

Manni, A., Chambers, M. J., & Pearson, O. H. Prolactin induces its own receptors in rat liver. *Endocrinology*, 1978, *103*, 2168-2171.

Marinari, K. T., & Moltz, H. Serum prolactin levels and vaginal cyclicity in concaveated and lactating female rats. *Physiology and Behavior*, 1978, *21*, 525-528.

Mata, L. J., & Urrutia, J. J. Intestinal colonization of breast-fed children in a rural area of low socioeconomic level. *Annals of the New York Academy of Science*, 1971, *176*, 93-109.

McNeish, A. S., Fleming, J., Turner, P., & Evans, N. Mucosal adherence of human enteropathogenic *Escherichia coli*. *Lancet*, 1975, *2*, 946-948.

Mekhjian, H. S., & Phillips, S. F. Perfusion of the canine colon with unconjugated bile acids. *Gastroenterology*, 1970, *59*, 120-129.

Moltz, H., & Leidahl, L. C. Bile, prolactin and the maternal pheromone. *Science*, 1977, *196*, 81-83.

Moltz, H., Leidahl, L. C. & Rowland, D. Prolongation of the maternal pheromone in the albino rat. *Physiology and Behavior*, 1974, *12*, 409-412.

Moltz, H., & Leon, M. Stimulus control of the maternal pheromone. *Physiology and Behavior* 1973, *10*, 69-71.

Norman, A., & Sjovall, J. Microbial transformation products of cholic acid in the rat. *Biochemica Biophysical Acto* 1958, *29*, 467-468. (a)

Norman, A., & Sjovall, J. On the transformation and enterohepatic circulation of cholic acid in the rat. *Journal Biological Chemistry*, 1958, *233*, 872-885. (b)

Norman, A., & Sjovall, J. Formation of lithocholic acid from chenodeoxycholic acid in the rat. *Acta Chemica Scandinavica*. 1960, *14*, 1815-1818.

Olivecrona, T., & Sjovall, J. Bile acids in rat portal blood. *Acta Physiologica Scandinovico*, 1959, *46*, 284-290.

Pitt, J., Barlow, B., & Heird, W. C. Protection against experimental necrotizing enterocolitis by maternal milk. I. Role of milk leukocytes. *Pediatric Research*, 1977, *11*, 906-909.

Posner, B. I., Kelly, P. A., & Friesen, H. G. Induction of a lactogenic receptor in rat liver: Influence of estrogen and the pituitary. *Proceedings of the National Academy of Science*, 1974, *71*, 2407-2410.

Posner, B. I., Kelly, P. A., & Friesen, H. G. Prolactin receptors in rat liver: Possible induction by prolactin. *Science*, 1975, *188*, 57-59.

Posner, B. I., Kelly, P. A., Shiu, R. P. C., & Friesen, H. G. Studies of insulin, GH and prolactin binding: Tissue distribution, species variation and characterization. *Endocrinology*, 1974, *95*, 521-531.

Rudbach, J. A., Anacker, R. L., Haskins, W. T., Johnson, A. G., Milner, K. C., & Ribi, E. Physical aspects of reversible inactivation of endotoxin. *Annals of the New York Academy of Science*, 1966, *133*, 629-643.

Shearman, D. J. C., Parkin, D. M., & McClelland, D. B. L. The demonstration and function of antibodies in the gastrointestinal tract. *Gut*, 1972, *13*, 483-499.

South, M. A. IgA in neonatal immunity. *Annals of the New York Academy of Science*, 1971, *176*, 40-48.

Stechschulte, D. J., & Austen, K. F. Immunoglobulins of rat colostrum. *Journal of Immunology* 1970, *104*. 1052-1062.

Touloukian, R. J., Posch, J. N., & Spencer, R. The pathogenesis of ischemic gastroenterocolitis of the neonate: Selective gut mucosal ischemia in asphyxiated neonatal piglets. *Journal of Pediatric Surgery* 1972, *7*, 194–205.

Weiner, J. M., & Lack, L. Bile salt absorption: Enterohepatic circulation. In C. F. Code (Ed.) *Handbook of physiology* (Section C), *Alimentary Canal* (Vol. 3). *Intestinal Absorption.* Washington, D.C.: American Physiological Society, 1968.

Author Index

Subject Index